CULTURAL CARING

The Human Side of Professional Learning Communities at Work®

Douglas Reeves
Robert Eaker

Solution Tree | Press

a division of Solution Tree

555 North Morton Street
Bloomington, IN 47404
800.733.6786 (toll free) / 812.336.7700
FAX: 812.336.7790

email: info@SolutionTree.com
SolutionTree.com

Visit **go.SolutionTree.com/PLCbooks** to download the free reproducibles in this book.

Printed in the United States of America

FSC
www.fsc.org
MIX
Paper | Supporting responsible forestry
FSC® C008955

Library of Congress Cataloging-in-Publication Data

Names: Reeves, Douglas B., 1953- author | Eaker, Robert author
Title: Cultural caring : the human side of professional learning communities at work / Douglas Reeves, Robert Eaker.
Description: Bloomington, IN : Solution Tree Press, [2025] | Includes bibliographical references and index.
Identifiers: LCCN 2024060129 (print) | LCCN 2024060130 (ebook) | ISBN 9798893740134 paperback | ISBN 9798893740141 ebook
Subjects: LCSH: School improvement programs | Caring | Group work in education | Team learning approach in education | Educational leadership
Classification: LCC LB2822.8 .R438 2025 (print) | LCC LB2822.8 (ebook) | DDC 371.2/07--dc23/eng/20250508
LC record available at https://lccn.loc.gov/2024060129
LC ebook record available at https://lccn.loc.gov/2024060130

Solution Tree
Jeffrey C. Jones, CEO
Edmund M. Ackerman, President

Solution Tree Press
Publisher: Kendra Slayton
Associate Publisher: Todd Brakke
Acquisitions Director: Hilary Goff
Editorial Director: Laurel Hecker
Art Director: Rian Anderson
Managing Editor: Sarah Ludwig
Copy Chief: Jessi Finn
Senior Production Editor: Suzanne Kraszewski
Copy Editor: Mark Hain
Proofreader: Elijah Oates
Cover and Text Designer: Fabiana Cochran
Content Development Specialist: Amy Rubenstein
Associate Editor: Elijah Oates
Editorial Assistant: Madison Chartier

Acknowledgments

My greatest debts are to the teachers and leaders I am privileged to see in classrooms around the world. They are the survivors—professionals who persist when so many others quit. They have struggled with learning loss and behavioral challenges, knowing that their reward may be decades hence. This book is the brainchild of my coauthor and colleague, Bob Eaker, who continues to keep the flame of Professional Learning Communities at Work® burning. When I am asked what I did for education, I will be able to say that I was a pretty good mathematics teacher. When Bob is asked that question, he will be able to say with Southern modesty, "Well, I tried to help thousands of teachers and educational leaders be more effective." I am profoundly grateful to our readers, including those who disagree with us. All any writer can ask for is a careful, if skeptical, reader. My grandmother, who was the first woman superintendent of schools in Illinois, taught us to "Do your best and forget the rest." These words are, so far, my best.

—*Douglas Reeves*

This book would never have come to life without the highly professional work of the entire staff at Solution Tree Press, particularly our editor Sue Kraszewski. My professional writing would not be possible absent the support and encouragement of my entire family—my wife, Star; my daughters, Robin and Carrie; and my grandchildren, Wyatt and Emma.

I have never believed in the concept of a self-made man or woman. We all stand on the shoulders of those who helped us along the way, both personally and professionally. In my case, I have been particularly blessed, since the number of people who have supported and encouraged me through the years is far too numerous to list. For each of them I am grateful.

—*Robert Eaker*

Solution Tree Press would like to thank the following reviewers:

Chris Bennett
Executive Director of Middle Schools & Accountability
Cleveland County Schools
Shelby, North Carolina

Ian Landy
Regional Principal of PIE
School District 47
Powell River, British Columbia, Canada

Louis Lim
Principal
Bur Oak Secondary School
Markham, Ontario, Canada

Ringnolda Jofee' Tremain
Chief Academic Officer
East Fort Worth Montessori Academy
Fort Worth, Texas

Visit **go.SolutionTree.com/PLCbooks** to download the free reproducibles in this book.

Table of Contents

Reproducibles are in italics.

Chapter 2

Chapter 3

Chapter 4

Chapter 9

Chapter 10

About the Authors

Douglas Reeves, PhD, is the author of more than forty books and more than one hundred articles on leadership and education. He has twice been named to the Harvard University Distinguished Authors Series and was named the Brock International Laureate for his contributions to education.

His career in professional learning led to him receiving a Contribution to the Field Award from the National Staff Development Council, now Learning Forward. His volunteer activities include FinishTheDissertation.org, providing free and noncommercial support for doctoral students, and *The SNAFU Review*, publishing the essays, poetry, stories, and artwork of disabled veterans. Dr. Reeves lives with his family in downtown Boston.

To learn more about Douglas Reeves's work, visit his blog at CreativeLeadership.net and follow @DouglasReeves on X.

Robert Eaker, EdD, is a professor emeritus at Middle Tennessee State University in Murfreesboro, where he also served as dean of the College of Education and interim vice president and provost. Dr. Eaker is a former fellow with the National Center for Effective Schools Research and Development. He has written widely on the issues of effective teaching, effective schools, helping teachers use research findings, high expectations for student achievement, and the Professional Learning Communities at Work process. Dr. Eaker has consulted with schools and school districts across North America and abroad, and is a frequent speaker at state and national conferences.

To learn more about Robert Eaker's work, visit AllThingsPLC.info.

To book Douglas Reeves or Robert Eaker for professional development, contact pd@SolutionTree.com.

Researcher, author, and speaker Zach Mercurio (2025) who specializes in leadership and positive organizational psychology writes:

> Today polls show that 30% of people report feeling invisible at work, 65% feel underappreciated, and close to 82% of workers feel lonely. Many of the workplace challenges currently plaguing leaders . . . can be traced to a growing mattering deficit. (p. 102)

This book seeks to address this mattering deficit within our schools. It is about caring; more specifically, it is about creating a *culture* of caring in classrooms, teams, schools, and school districts, for both students and adults.

Our friend and colleague Maria Nielsen, a former teacher, reflects on what it means to experience a culture of caring in school (Solution Tree, 2025). She recalls an encounter with one of her former students where the student told her the following story:

> I'll never forget the day you cried. It was a day when Ben was absent, and you pulled all of us ten-year-olds over to the carpet. You told us a little bit about Ben and some of his struggles, and you cried, and you asked us to take care of Ben. . . . I want you to know that we took care of Ben as a class through middle school and all the way through high school.

Through sharing this story, Maria reminds teachers not to forget the power they have to change the lives of students. She writes, "in addition to bringing students academic value, we should be teaching them about life, and we do that through the things we speak to them about and the way we model our own behaviors—how to show up and take care of each other and how to be good humans" (Solution Tree, 2025, p. 21).

Introduction

This book is about the human side of the Professional Learning Communities (PLCs) at Work® process. We recognize the importance of the structural changes required for effectively implementing the PLC at Work process, but we also recognize that without cultural caring for both students and adults, schools are unlikely to reach the full potential of the process. *Culture* is the total of everyone in the organization's behavior—their habits—day in and day out. By *cultural caring*, we mean creating a culture of kindness and concern for others. Janel Keating, former superintendent of the White River School District in Buckley, Washington, frequently reminded her administrators, faculty, and support staff that parents want three things from school for their kids. They want them to be safe, both physically and psychologically, they want them to learn, and they also want their child to feel special—to be in a school and classrooms in which they feel that the adults care for them as individuals. Janel referred to this as the "standard of care" that a school promises to parents and the larger school community.

We advocate cultural caring in schools that touches the emotions. By *touching the emotions*, we mean having a strong, positive emotional effect. The ideas, concepts, and practices we present in the following chapters are based on the premise that the human side of the PLC at Work process has not received the emphasis it deserves.

Although the PLC at Work process is a proven approach for increasing student and adult learning, we can't forget why we should *want* to undertake the hard work of implementing the PLC at Work process in the first place. We should want to do so because we care for the intellectual, physical, social, and emotional learning—learning in the broadest sense—of each student. We should also want to implement the PLC at Work process to its fullest because we care about our colleagues and their professional and personal success.

The PLC at Work process and the supporting resources, including *Learning by Doing: A Handbook for Professional Learning Communities at Work* by Richard DuFour and colleagues (2024), present the *what*, the *why*, and the *how* of the PLC process. However, creating a culture in which everyone *wants* to do the right work for the right reasons is a difficult challenge that often goes unaddressed. Why should we *want* to do the work of a PLC? Because we care enough for our students and colleagues to embed best practices into every aspect of school culture. This includes everyone from the school board to the support staff—there are no exceptions!

The ideas and practices we present in this book assume that it is futile to undertake improvement initiatives—even those with the best of intentions and hard work—without a focus on creating a culture of caring. Simply put, genuine caring is a primary motivator for both students and adults (Eaker & Keating, 2015; Hattie, 2009; Marzano, Pickering, & Pollock, 2001). Because cultural change is so difficult, many settle for something less; they choose to focus, almost exclusively, on the structural aspects of schooling—things such as policies, procedures, organizational charts, job descriptions, and rules. Of course, these structural aspects of schooling are necessary, but by themselves, they are inadequate. Hence, the term "PLC Lite" is increasingly used to describe schools that call themselves PLCs but have in fact only added a thin veneer of structural change that covers the same traditional culture that has characterized the school for years (DuFour & Reeves, 2016).

Because We Care: Seeking, Trying, and Using Best Practices

Best practice is generally revealed through the work of educational researchers. Referring to particular educational practices as "best practices" has become somewhat of a fad. After all, who would be opposed to best practice? Shouldn't best practice be just *practice that works*? Some educators may resist best practice because they believe it is theoretical rather than practical and that the research does not apply to their specific school setting. For example, a teacher might ask, "How can research conducted in urban schools possibly be helpful to my small rural school?" On the other hand, research-based practices that also have been *practitioner proven* are much more credible with educators.

We support the use of *action research*. According to Mike Mattos, Richard DuFour, Rebecca DuFour, Robert Eaker, and Thomas W. Many (2016), action research in a PLC means "we are willing to try new practices and procedures and then measure their impact on student learning to determine if the change was beneficial" (p. 6). What makes action research so compelling is that it is done within the school setting so that teachers and administrators who may be distrustful of the effectiveness of outside research will know that these professional practices work within their particular setting and with their students. When creating a culture of caring, it is imperative that teachers and leaders embrace an ethic of action research so they can conclude, "We know this works here, and it is worthy of implementation." If a practice doesn't work in a specific district or school, action research provides the shared knowledge to understand why the practice did not have the desired effects.

Action research allows adults in learning organizations to continually learn. This adult learning leads to increased student learning. A major theme of this book is that both student learning and adult learning are more likely to occur in schools that reflect, in multiple, tangible ways, a culture of caring (Audisio, Taylor-Perryman, Tasker, & Steinberg, 2023; Kruger, Godley, & Heavey, 2021; Ryu, Walls, & Seashore Louis, 2020). When we refer to adult learning, we are not only referring to teachers; adult learning refers to everyone—administrators, teachers, the entire support staff, parents, and the larger community in which the school exists. A bus driver or server in the lunch line can support a caring culture or, sadly, reflect just the opposite attitude.

PLCs Reflect Best Practice: Implementing the PLC at Work Process

In our decades-long work in schools as both educators, administrators, and educational consultants, we have come to understand that one of the most effective ways of ensuring best practice and improving adult and student learning is to implement the PLC at Work process (DuFour et al., 2024) with fidelity and specificity. The efficacy of the PLC at Work process has been well documented by researchers and practitioners alike (Cottingham, Hough, & Myung, 2023; Hanson et al., 2021; Read On Arizona, 2024; Solution Tree, 2024a–j). Embedding PLC practices deep into every aspect of school culture requires an emphasis on cultural caring.

Mike Schmoker (2004) reminds us that "clarity precedes competence" (p. 85). Schmoker's admonition is especially true with PLC at Work implementation. Before we can fully understand how creating a culture of caring is indispensable in a PLC at Work, we must be clear on what the PLC at Work process is and how it works. Richard DuFour and colleagues (2024) define a PLC as follows:

> An ongoing process in which educators work collaboratively in recurring cycles of collective inquiry and action research to achieve better results for the students they serve. PLCs operate under the assumption that the key to improved learning for students is continuous job-embedded learning for educators. (p. 2)

As helpful as this definition is, it does not articulate the structural and cultural shifts that occur when a more traditional school undertakes the journey to function as a PLC. The foundation of a PLC is based on three structural and cultural shifts.

1. A shift from a focus on teaching—the coverage of curricula—to a focus on the learning of each student, skill by skill
2. A shift from a structure and culture of teacher isolation, where teachers work primarily by themselves, to teachers working in a collaborative culture, where team members hold each other mutually accountable
3. A shift from intentions to a focus on results where success is based on evidence of student learning

These three foundational shifts form the framework for the day-to-day work that occurs in a PLC. Recognizing that today's schools are complex organizations and educators are asked to do more than ever before, PLCs ask four essential questions to guide the *core* work, but not the only work, that provides a sharp focus on learning, day in and day out (DuFour et al., 2024).

1. What is essential for all students to learn in each subject, grade level, course, and unit of instruction, and what does this learning look like if students are successful?
2. How will we know whether or not students are learning—student by student, and skill by skill?
3. How does the school respond when students struggle with their learning?
4. How does the school extend the learning for students who demonstrate proficiency?

Clarity on the PLC at Work process, the three structural and cultural shifts, and the four questions that guide the core work in schools and teams provides educational leaders with a target that beckons—a way of thinking and doing. Certainly, most educators are in favor of school improvement; it's just the *actions* necessary to improve schools that many are opposed to. To some degree, this opposition is understandable, since, simply put, significant and sustainable change is difficult.

Closing the Knowing and Action Gap: Caring Enough to Act

We have authored this book as a call to action. While becoming informed, or even convinced, is necessary, without the necessary accompanying actions, very little, if anything, changes. We believe the vast majority of educators entered our profession with the best of intentions for their students, their colleagues, and the health of our profession. However, intentions are not enough. We must act; we must do! The challenges we place before our readers are these: Care enough to gain shared knowledge, care enough to develop shared commitments, and then care enough to act.

When we are ill and see a physician, we expect that the doctor, a licensed professional, knows and *will use* the latest and most effective practices when treating us. They will go beyond simply being aware of best practices; they will care enough to use them! Professionals use best practices because they care enough to make sure that what they do aligns with the best information available at the time. Since new knowledge is constantly being generated, professionals must be continually learning. For educators, this means continually seeking best practices and then trying out those practices (through action research) because we care about our students and colleagues and the larger community we serve. This focus on cultural caring should be a defining characteristic of schools.

Expanding the Focus From Test Scores to Learning

Because education is a helping profession, educators have unique expectations placed on them. At the forefront of these expectations is student learning, and we believe the current state of American public education reflects a far-too-narrow view of student learning. Since the No Child Left Behind Act of 2001 (No Child Left Behind, 2002), student learning has been defined by how well students perform compared to others on high-stakes, commercially developed tests. For more than a quarter of a century, the United States education system has been mired in a testing culture. While seldom stated, doing well on state tests has incrementally morphed into the primary mission of many, if not most, schools.

Our work is based on a much broader view of student learning. While norm-referenced assessments of student learning have a role to play, we believe schools are effective when students have learned the essentials that will enable them to live healthy, intellectually stimulating, psychologically satisfying, and successful lives. Many important things that have a huge influence on success and happiness beyond school cannot be measured, such as caring for others. Hence, we assume that schools cannot accomplish their learning mission unless they have created a culture of caring. In other words, we care about our students' *quality* of life—not merely how they perform on tests. We also care about our colleagues' quality of life so as not to leave them working in isolation by themselves.

About This Book

The best practices that are the focus of this book support a culture of caring for both students and educators.

- Chapter 1 explores the link between caring school environments and motivation and encourages concrete steps leaders can take to promote care and support in their schools.
- Chapter 2 broadens the discussion of motivation to detail the work of the individual classroom teacher to promote care and support.
- Chapter 3 introduces the importance of feedback to sustain a committed and caring environment and describes authentic feedback, including two tools for leaders to use.
- Chapter 4 addresses the need for student support beyond the school walls and how teachers can help by assuming positive motivations from students and parents and encouraging skills such as delayed gratification to support students beyond the classroom.

- Chapter 5 examines how leaders can provide support and resources to teachers in their classroom roles that promote a caring culture.
- Chapter 6 focuses on the impact teamwork and collaboration have in creating a caring culture in PLCs.
- Chapter 7 identifies key leadership qualities that best foster caring cultures.
- Chapter 8 looks at how governing boards can support school leaders as they implement caring practices.
- Chapter 9 discusses leadership decisions to drive actions that protect and enforce a caring culture.
- Chapter 10 broadens the scope of a caring culture, first to the local community and then nationally.

At the conclusion of each chapter, you will find questions for discussion that you can reflect on individually or discuss with collaborative groups within your school or district.

As you begin reading this book, consider the following questions: What does *caring* mean to you as someone who provides a caring environment? What does it mean to you as someone who receives caring?

CHAPTER 1

The Caring Imperative

I've learned that people will forget what you said, people will forget what you did, but people will never forget how you made them feel.

—Maya Angelou

In our work in schools, we have found that it is rare for people to oppose the idea of a caring culture in schools. The challenge in creating a caring culture is not one of *convincing* people that it is the right thing to do; rather, the challenge is *doing* it—acting in planned, meaningful, purposeful ways with specificity and fidelity. The question is, do we care enough to do the things necessary to create a caring culture, and why doesn't it bother us if we don't?

The Role of Feelings and Emotion

The desire to improve organizational effectiveness is evident in many change initiatives. Examples include modifications to an organization's framework, such as adjustments to the chain of command, resource allocation, and the assignment of new roles and responsibilities, to name a few. These examples constitute structural changes, which have been the goal of improving effectiveness since the early 1900s. In his influential book *The Principles of Scientific Management*, Frederick Winslow Taylor (1911) presents ideas based on the understanding that improving organizational effectiveness is inextricably linked to improving organizational *efficiency*, and organizational efficiency is primarily improved by refining the *structural* aspects of organizations. In Taylor's time, employees' human needs were not given much, if any, consideration (DuFour et al., 2024).

This view of organizational improvement changed dramatically with the work of Elton Mayo, an Australian professor at the Harvard Business School (Hendry, 2013). In the 1920s, using Taylor's (1911) framework for traditional approaches to improvement, Mayo and his associates were involved in traditional time and motion studies at the Western Electric plant in Hawthorne, Illinois (Hendry, 2013). One particular area they investigated was the effect of various lighting conditions on worker productivity. Their findings changed the way organizations of all kinds, worldwide, came to view organizational improvement.

Mayo and his colleagues discovered that lighting conditions, by themselves, had no effect on productivity, since productivity improved whenever the lighting conditions were changed either up or down. After additional years of investigation, including interviews with employees, it seemed that productivity was impacted less by working conditions than by the affective aspect of employee relations (Hendry, 2013).

Employees in the study felt important because of the attention being paid to them and their views. John Hendry (2013) sums up the primary findings of the Western Electric studies by writing, "Feelings mattered, and wherever managers took a personal interest in the workers, made them feel important, and generated a mutually supportive and cooperative environment, output was enhanced" (p. 65). We suggest that current school-improvement efforts in the United States could benefit greatly if leaders moved beyond mere structural changes (policies, procedures, practices, job descriptions, and so on) and enhanced the attention paid to the human side of school improvement—in other words, by touching the emotions and showing genuine caring for students and adults in the school community.

What We *Do*—Not What We *Say*

Culture is the total of everyone in the organization's behavior—their habits—day in and day out. Terry Deal and Allen Kennedy (1982) further define culture as the sum total of how we do things. The key word in Deal and Kennedy's (1982) definition is *do*. Many schools and districts operate under a very different assumption—the assumption that culture is what they proclaim: "We're a learning community," "Every student is a winner," "Learning for all," and so on. In many school districts, classrooms, teams, and support staff offices, there is a gap between what people say they *believe* and what they actually *do*. For example, schools that have effective collaborative teacher teams will have 100 percent participation by every team member, who share authentic examples of student work, ask colleagues for help with especially challenging student learning objectives, and offer support for colleagues. But in the other schools, meetings with the same label of "collaborative teacher teams" have one person doing all the talking while everyone else listens. It is just another traditional faculty meeting with a different label.

In *The Knowing-Doing Gap: How Smart Companies Turn Knowledge Into Action*, Jeffrey Pfeffer and Robert I. Sutton (2000) explore the gap between what we know and what we do by posing the question, "Why does knowledge of what needs to be done so frequently fail to result in action or behavior that is consistent with that knowledge?" (p. 4). In creating a culture of caring in schools, we would ask a similar but equally important question: "Why is our *caring behavior* often so inconsistent with what we *say*?" Our response: *Culture is what we do—not what we say!*

We contend there is no lack of recognition about the importance of a caring culture in schools. We often speak of it and read it on our posters, signs, bulletins, flags, and even lapel pins. Such pronouncements are inspiring and motivating on the surface. However, we should ask what specific *behaviors* in schools reflect a deep, rich culture of caring. Can we clearly articulate what a caring culture would look like at the district, school, team, and individual classroom levels for both students and adults?

Imagine that an investigative television program or podcast has been granted permission to spend a month in your school filming and collecting footage for a show about the current state of American education. After a month of filming, during the editing process, what behaviors would the directors and producers see as they review their footage? For example, if the school proclaims, in multiple ways, that they value a caring culture, what filmed behaviors would indicate the degree to which a caring culture actually exists?

Motivation and Caring

Mayo's findings ignited a plethora of research into the psychological aspects of human motivation (Hendry, 2013). Perhaps the most highly recognized is the work of Abraham Maslow. Certainly, most students of the social sciences are exposed to Maslow (1954) and his groundbreaking work *Motivation and Personality*. In his well-known hierarchy of needs, Maslow emphasizes the relationship between humans' psychological needs and motivation. Subsequent years of research have only reinforced Maslow's thesis that students and adults alike are motivated primarily by the meeting of psychological needs, which include the need for belonging, love, and esteem, all of which are met by being cared for or caring about others (Kenrick, Griskevicius, Neuberg, & Schaller, 2011).

Simon Sinek (2009b) reminds us that there are only two ways to influence human behavior: "You can manipulate it or you can inspire it" (p. 17). We believe that it is impossible to inspire others in the absence of genuine, meaningful caring. In short, we believe that motivation in schools is linked directly to the degree in which school leaders touch the emotions of both students and adults. Daniel Goleman, Richard E. Boyatzis, and Anne McKee (2002) got it right with their observation:

> Great leaders move us. They ignite our passion and inspire the best in us. When we try to explain why they are so effective, we speak of strategy, vision, or powerful ideas. But, the reality is much more primal. Great leadership works through emotions. (p. 3)

We must also consider how schools, however unintentionally, demotivate students and staff members. Students can be demotivated by factors such as fear of failure and low self-efficacy. For example, in some classrooms, students enthusiastically participate, knowing that a wrong answer will not be met with shame and humiliation, but rather will be an opportunity to learn and grow. But in many schools, only right answers are praised, especially when teachers call only on students who already know the right answer. That is not real learning. Further, students are demotivated in a classroom culture characterized by harshness of a teacher's verbal tone or a teacher's lack of interest in their students. For teachers, demotivating can include a workload that is so overwhelming it leads to burnout, large class sizes, lack of resources, lack of administrative support, lack of professional development opportunities, and punitive accountability measures, to name a few.

A caring culture allows educators to turn around demotivating factors. For example, when calling on students, teachers can use equity sticks or other random calling devices to ensure that every student has the opportunity to contribute to the class, and, when they respond with an incorrect answer or an honest admission that they just do not know the right answer, caring teachers will coach them from misunderstanding to deep understanding. They might be prompted to "phone a friend," answer a question with a question, or provide a partial answer, strategies that provide emotional and psychological safety (Reeves, 2021b).

To counter demotivating factors for teachers, leaders can demonstrate a culture of caring by observing and listening to the teachers' working conditions and by organizing teachers into high-performing collaborative teams. Often teachers feel overwhelmed and like they are asked to do more than is possible. Working as part of a team provides teachers with a support system where things seem more doable and teachers feel supported.

Emotional and Psychological Safety

When we think of safety in schools, many of us think of physical safety. Parents expect their children will be safe in school, and teachers expect that they will be safe as well. Given the increasing number of school shootings in the United States every year (Korhonen, 2024), it is understandable that when thinking of safety in schools, the *physical* safety of students and adults is most likely the first thing that comes to mind. Everyone, both within and outside of schools, should make the physical safety of students and adults the top priority of a school's structure and culture.

We should recognize, however, that the concept of cultural safety in schools goes far beyond physical safety. School leaders must also focus on developing a safe emotional and psychological culture for everyone. Creating such a culture begins by recognizing that many students and adults fear certain aspects of schooling.

The recognition that school can be a fearful place is not new. In his classic work, *How Children Fail*, John Holt (1964) writes the following:

> What is most surprising of all is how much fear there is in school. Why is so little said about it? Perhaps most people do not recognize fear in children when they see it. They can read the grossest signs of fear, they know what the trouble is when a child clings howling to his mother, but the subtler signs of fear escapes them. It is these signs, in children's faces, voices, and gestures, in their movements and ways of working, that tell me plainly that most children in school are scared most of the time, many of them very scared. (p. 49)

In *Fearless Schools*, Douglas Reeves (2021b) notes that neuroscience provides ample evidence that fear is the enemy of learning. When students (and adults) are fearful, they cannot learn. Students may fear the embarrassment of not being accepted by their peers—of being left out—not only by students but also by the school itself. The need for belonging or being included is strong, and many students and adults fear being left out or rejected (Edmondson, 2023).

Students might feel they are not safe emotionally when they fear being teased, especially by their peers. Many students fear going to school because they are afraid other students might make fun of them, or that a teacher might belittle them in front of the class. Researcher Alexis Wiggins (2018) shadowed high school students, sitting in the same desks, eating in the same cafeteria, and waiting in the same lines. She found that for the vast majority of the school day, students endured the sarcastic remarks of teachers. While these remarks were intended to be funny, students were deeply wounded by the sarcasm.

Fear of bullying is a major obstruction to emotional safety for students. Bullying is not a new phenomenon and can take different forms. Students can be afraid of bullying by other students or by a teacher, administrator, or a member of the support staff. It can happen at school or at home. Students need feedback about their learning, behavior, and attitude. This feedback from staff members can become a form of bullying when used inappropriately. Students can feel bullied when they hear often that they are a failure and cannot improve.

The widespread use of social media has added a new and frightening dimension to bullying. A 2022 report by the Pew Research Center (Vogels, 2022) notes that nearly half (46 percent) of teenagers between the ages thirteen and seventeen have experienced some form of bullying. Social media has become a source of stress, anxiety, and depression (Haidt, 2024). Students are preoccupied with their "likes" and other indicators of social affirmation, and as a result they grow distant from human interaction. MIT Professor Sherry Turkle (2015) argues that students need "human time" with real conversations that are not assisted by texts or email, but that require face-to-face, voice-to-voice communication. Without the practice of human time, she argues, students can excel in every measure except those that are necessary to succeed in life and the workplace. Schools can provide that critical human time that supports emotional and psychological safety.

A caring culture reflects an understanding that the degree to which students and adults succeed depends to a great extent on how their school addresses the need for emotional safety through specific policies, procedures, behaviors, and attitudes. Everyone learns what the school values by seeing what its leaders address and what they give high priority to. A true caring culture goes beyond recognizing the need for emotional and psychological safety to developing policies, procedures, and plans (including training) that prioritize identifying what creates a culture that allows fear in the school and eliminating it.

One of the most visible ways to support emotional and psychological safety is through planned forums with students to discuss various topics related to such safety. For example, bullying, testing anxiety, peer pressure, addressing failure, and the role social media plays in relationships are obvious topics for discussion. These discussions help everyone understand that their fears and anxieties are not necessarily unique. More importantly, the forums communicate a larger message: The school knows the importance of emotional and psychological safety and is addressing the issue in multiple ways.

Schools communicate high priorities by what their leaders are willing to confront (DuFour et al., 2024; DuFour & Eaker, 1998). It does little good for a school to proclaim that certain behaviors are harmful and should not occur, then ignore these very behaviors when they occur. This is often the case when a school has taken a strong stance against bullying of any sort, yet they refuse to confront the behavior of a teacher who frequently bullies students or perhaps even other adults. When the school community sees bullying or other inappropriate behaviors being confronted, the message that emotional safety is important is heard loud and clear, and more importantly, the message is *believed*.

Questions for Discussion

This chapter explored the link between caring school environments and motivation, encouraging concrete steps leaders can take to promote care and support in their schools. Use the "Caring Imperative Questions for Discussion" in the reproducible on page 17 to reflect on your school or district.

Caring Imperative Questions for Discussion

1. How have your school and district closed the "knowing-doing gap"—that is, how are your stated priorities consistent with the actions of teachers and leaders?
2. How do your school and district respond to bullying? Are these responses different when addressing student incidents (bullying on the playground, for example) and adult incidents (like bullying in a board meeting)? How do you set boundaries for teachers, administrators, parents, and community members when they cross the line from strongly held opinions to threats and bullying?
3. What are the signs that your students are emotionally safe? What are the signs that they are not emotionally safe, and what steps can you take to guarantee their safety?
4. Have you shadowed a student, as Alexis Wiggins did, and really walked a few miles in a student's shoes? What did you notice? If you have not done so, what would be necessary for you to shadow a student?

CHAPTER 2

Caring Classrooms

I have come to a frightening conclusion. I am the decisive element in the classroom. It is my personal approach that creates the climate. It is my daily mood that makes the weather. As a teacher I possess tremendous power to make a child's life miserable or joyous. I can be a tool of torture or an instrument of inspiration. I can humiliate or humor, hurt or heal. In all situations, it is my response that decides whether a crisis will be escalated or de-escalated, and a child humanized or dehumanized.

—Haim G. Ginott

While district and school cultures provide the broader foundation for a caring culture, the classroom is the *primary* focus of cultural caring. Since students spend the majority of their school day in classrooms, it is impossible for students to experience a high degree of caring without caring experiences in class. Importantly, the degree that a caring culture is present in classrooms will determine, to a great extent, the likelihood of student success. In *The Art and Science of Teaching*, researcher Robert J. Marzano (2007) contends, "Arguably the quality of the relationship teachers have with students is the keystone of effective management and perhaps even the entirety of teaching" (p. 149). The prevailing worship of high-stakes norm-referenced testing focuses on *effects* (test scores) and not on *causes* (relationships and trust).

Student learning is at the core of every effective classroom, and the degree to which teachers exhibit positive caring relationships with students has a major effect on student achievement (Rimm-Kaufman & Sandilos, 2025; Saphier, Haley-Speca, & Gower, 2008). A caring classroom culture also affects classroom climate and management. Rosa Hernandez Sheets and Geneva Gay (1996) contend that the root causes of many behavioral issues in classrooms lie in how students and teachers relate to one another. According to EdTrust (2021), "strong relationships provide a foundation for student engagement, belonging, and, ultimately, learning. The more high-quality relationships students have with their teachers, the better their engagement in school."

The foundation of a caring classroom culture rests with connecting what we are doing to why we are doing it, and the why in a caring community is the fact that the teacher cares for students. Sinek (2009b) contends that "people don't buy *what* you do, they buy *why* you do it" (p. 64). Sinek's observation explains why caring is such a powerful motivator.

Given the attention paid to testing in schools, it is reasonable to assume that the primary motivation for what occurs in schools and classrooms is students getting high scores on state and other high-stakes tests. While doing well on state tests is important, test results should not be the primary reason educators do what they do. The message must be that we do what we do because we care so much. Our students must understand that we are doing all that's within our power to ensure that each of them learns the things essential for their future happiness, health, and intellectual success (DuFour et al., 2024).

Embracing Meaningful Accountability

Rejecting accountability based exclusively on test scores does not mean we are opposed to meaningful school accountability. We insist, however, that as a society, we get accountability right. The Every Student Succeeds Act (2015) explicitly gives states and school systems the flexibility to include far more than test scores in their accountability measures, including the manner in which schools build caring relationships with students (DuFour, Reeves, & DuFour, 2018). We insist that accountability can be a constructive force for educational improvement, especially when part of the accountability system is the annual sharing of effective practices that teachers know work with their culture, schedule, budget, and collective bargaining agreements (Reeves, 2016). In *Learning by Doing*, DuFour and colleagues (2024) provide the following examples of how schools can connect what we do with the caring why.

- The reason we, as teachers, work in collaborative teams is that we care for our students and want them to learn. The evidence is clear: Collaborative teaming is a powerful tool for enhancing student learning.
- The reason we, as a team of teachers, clarify the specific skills, knowledge, and dispositions essential for every student to learn is that we know that clearly articulating the essential learning for all students in each grade, course, unit, and lesson will increase the likelihood of student learning.
- We, as individual teachers and as a team, monitor the learning of each student on a frequent and timely basis because we care for our students and want them to be successful learners. The evidence is clear: Assessing student learning during the teaching and learning process is more effective than relying primarily on end-of-unit or end-of-course summative assessments (Stulberg, 2021).
- Because we care for students' learning success, we have put in place a system to ensure every student

receives additional time and support and extension of their learning.

Connecting the What With the Why

Connecting what we do with the fact that we care is more than important—it is the pillar on which more specific behaviors rest. However, it is not the only pillar. A caring classroom is guided by valuing empathy and compassion. Caring teachers are empathetic; they can view the classroom through the lens of their students. They can recall what it was like to be a student like the ones they are teaching. Because they can remember how they felt themselves and their own fears and concerns, they can be compassionate, supportive, and creative teachers.

When teachers share with their students memories of their own experiences as a student, it communicates a sense of understanding, and it is impossible to be an empathetic and compassionate teacher without a sense of understanding. Consider, for example, a teacher sharing her experience as a student when she was required to rewrite an essay or when she had to resubmit a lab report three times. Sharing this experience of perceived failure and the resulting persistence provides a model of resilience students need.

Being an empathetic teacher and understanding what it's like to be a student helps teachers think about how they can effectively plan for teaching that builds solid relationships with students and has a profound impact on learning and behavior. For example, when thinking about a specific lesson, teachers can ask themselves, "If I were a student in this class, how could I best learn these instructional objectives?" In other words, caring and empathetic teachers enhance their students' likelihood of success because they view the classroom and lessons through their students' eyes.

Unfortunately, not all students believe they can learn what is being asked of them. A caring classroom is characterized by encouragement and support. While the quality of feedback students receive is important, the effect of feedback alone will be severely limited unless coupled with encouragement and support. One of the great mysteries of formal education is that there is almost unanimous recognition that students learn at different rates and in different ways. Yet, in many schools, when students do not learn at the same rate and do not meet arbitrary and artificial standards, they are labeled as failures. A caring teacher connects frequent and timely formative assessments with feedback. The teacher connects feedback with encouragement and additional time and support, communicating all of this to students in ways that indicate genuine caring.

Caring by Doing: Learning Together

It's unlikely any educator would express opposition to the importance of caring for students. As we wrote earlier, the issue with developing a caring culture is seldom one of *convincing*, but rather one of *doing*, and doing implies specificity: What behaviors communicate caring? Teachers in a school that functions as a PLC have the benefit of being members of a high-performing team. Team members can brainstorm and share ideas. They can experiment and determine behaviors and routines that have a positive impact on students' attitudes and behaviors, and subsequently, their learning. In short, they benefit by learning together.

Teachers can share with their fellow team members their ways of creating a caring classroom culture. Teams can also learn caring behaviors by engaging in collective inquiry, seeking out research findings and ideas about what works. For example, Robert J. Marzano (2007) organizes caring behaviors into these eight action steps.

1. **Know something about each student.** For example, let students know you are interested in them by asking questions about themselves. Some sample questions include the following.
    a. "Where were you born?"
    b. "How many brothers and sisters do you have?"
    c. "What hobbies are you interested in?"
2. **Engage in behaviors that indicate affection for each student.** For example, meet students at the door and, to the degree possible, greet them by name. At the beginning of the year, take photos of each student and display them,

along with students' thoughts about the class. For students who feel alienated, take time to attend an after-school function in which the student is participating, such as a sporting event.

3. **Bring student interests into the content and personalize learning activities.** For example, weave student interests into lessons and involve students in meaningful and relevant ways as much as possible.
4. **Engage in physical behaviors that communicate interest in students.** For example, when appropriate, smile at students. When talking with students, look them in the eyes. Demonstrate interest in what students have to say.
5. **Use humor when appropriate.** For example, when appropriate, engage in playful banter with students. Use appropriate jokes or cartoons, or a funny story at the beginning of class. Laugh at yourself, and laugh with (but not at) students.
6. **Consistently enforce positive and negative consequences.** For example, establish learning goals, rules, and procedures, along with positive and negative consequences related to the rules and procedures. In other words, develop clear and appropriate ways of doing things in the class and, importantly, stick to those procedures, rules, and consequences consistently.
7. **Project a sense of emotional objectivity.** For example, provide students with a consistent tone. (This does not mean the teacher never expresses emotions.) Behave in a way that communicates care and concern equally for every student. Teachers should monitor their own thoughts and emotions. They can do so by engaging in practices like mentally reflecting on their emotional reaction to each student.

   In addition, teachers who have negative feelings about particular students should determine the specific characteristics or past events that are causing negative thoughts. When possible, try to reframe student behavior that is causing negative emotions and attempt to view the student's behavior from another point of view, perhaps giving the student the benefit of the doubt.

8. **Maintain a cool exterior.** For example, a teacher should avoid extremes by guarding against behaviors such as pointing a finger or shaking a fist at offending students, raising their voice toward a student, glaring or staring at the student, or ridiculing students. Remember, ignoring students is a hurtful behavior as well.

   Instead, teachers should speak directly at students in a calm and respectful tone. Look directly at students without glaring at them. Maintain an appropriate distance from students and have either a neutral or positive facial expression. Focus on the students' behaviors as opposed to their motives.

Jon Saphier, Mary Ann Haley-Speca, and Robert Gower (2008) offer similar examples of teacher behaviors that communicate a caring classroom culture. They report that when students were interviewed about their relationships with teachers, they repeatedly mentioned teacher behaviors that fall into six categories.

1. **Providing acknowledgment:** For example, students repeatedly mentioned teachers greeting them when they enter the classroom or pass them in the hall or welcoming them back when they have been absent. Students also identified teachers maintaining eye contact with them during whole-group instruction, encouraging them to participate, and clarifying when students seem confused. Students felt that ensuring that everyone is heard and acknowledged during class discussions was also important.
2. **Communicating value:** Teachers communicate value by doing the following.
   a. *Showing interest*—Teachers who show interest know students' names and use their names when

talking with them in and out of class. They know what students' cultures or neighborhoods are like. They ask about students' interests and strengths. They want to know how each student's day is going. They inquire about a student if they have been out of school. They ask students what is bothering them when their facial expressions communicate something is wrong. They make connections to the world of students.

b. *Being a good listener*—Teachers who are good listeners listen carefully without interrupting. They acknowledge what students are saying and ask for more details if they are unsure. They make sure they understand students and pose reflective questions that encourage further thinking.

c. *Having high expectations and persistence*—Teachers communicate high expectations to students about their academic performance, work habits, behavior, and so on. They emphasize persistence by reminding students when they need extra help, making time to work with students, and trying alternate approaches to help students learn when the way being used isn't working.

d. *Reestablishing contact*—After strongly correcting a student, teachers reestablish contact on a more positive note, thus reducing tension between themselves and the student.

e. *Being accessible*—Teachers make time for students outside of class—not for punishment, but in ways that students can see the teacher cares. Being accessible is more than merely saying, "Stop by after school if you need help." Many students who most need help have after-school responsibilities, including sibling care and jobs. School leaders must create time during the school day for students to contact teachers and get help immediately, not at the end of the semester when they are facing an academic crisis.

3. **Showing respect:** Teachers can show respect for students by treating them as valuable and capable. They give students opportunities to express their opinions. They involve students in appropriate ways about decisions that will directly affect students. They are courteous and respectful when interacting with students. They demonstrate an interest in what is going on in each student's world. They discipline students privately. They do not denigrate students. They are honest and fair with students and inspire students by being a role model for what is expected from them.
4. **Being fair:** Teachers let students know what is expected rather than surprise them. They thoroughly explain how they will grade student work. They grade students fairly. They have reasonable rules that they apply consistently. They don't make unfair assumptions about students.
5. **Being real:** Teachers share relevant and appropriate information about their own lives and experiences with students as well as appropriate personal anecdotes.
6. **Using humor and fun:** Teachers recognize that students need to have fun. They don't try to be a comedian, but they recognize humorous events when they occur. They laugh with students at appropriate times and include fun activities when appropriate and in appropriate ways.

There is no definitive list of teacher behaviors for creating a caring classroom culture. However, strategies such as those listed here serve as a resource for individual teachers to reflect on their own behaviors and the quality of a caring culture in their classroom. Teams can use the list to start deep, rich conversations about ensuring that their behaviors are congruent with their professed desire for a caring classroom culture.

Since many of the teachers on a school's staff or individual team have children of their own, the ultimate question for discussing, reflecting, and committing to a standard of care is, "Would every procedure, policy, lesson, and interaction that occurs in every classroom be good enough for our own children?" This question can be more than a mere cliché; it can be used as a standard of care that each administrator, teacher, or member of the support staff makes to the parents of each student and to the larger community (Eaker & Keating, 2012, 2015).

Having High Expectations

Developing a culture of deep caring depends on a culture of high expectations for all students and adults alike. It is impossible to have a caring culture without a culture of high expectations. The two are intertwined.

Developing a culture of high expectations is much more than merely requiring more of students or changing grading practices. At its core, having high expectations refers to inferences educators make about the future academic success of students (Good & Brophy, 1990). High expectations are frequently categorized in two ways: (1) sustaining expectations and (2) self-fulfilling prophecies. The sustaining expectation effect reinforces and maintains existing behaviors, the result being a barrier to change. On the other hand, self-fulfilling prophecies encourage change because the beliefs that teachers hold can cause students' success or lack thereof to become a reality (Cooper & Good, 1983; Eaker & Keating, 2015).

High expectations for cultural caring begin with the adults in the school. When thinking about the importance of high expectations, it is not unusual to immediately think of students' academic performance. Embedding a caring culture instead depends first on the adults having high expectations for themselves, both individually and as a group.

Educators must consider what shared *commitments* they are prepared to make to ensure their students succeed at the highest level possible. Shared commitments are the core of high expectations because they represent what schools are prepared to do to enhance student success. And, because expectations are part of every organization, shared commitments to certain behaviors and attitudes must be collaboratively developed, articulated, embedded, monitored, celebrated, and continually reinforced at every level.

Every teacher we know believes that their classrooms are full of high expectations. How can they verify that claim? The best way we know is a core PLC at Work practice: collaborative scoring (DuFour et al., 2024). When faculty members look at a piece of anonymous student work and come to very different conclusions about how that work should be scored, it becomes clear that expectations are not an objective and consistent judgment, but rather an idiosyncratic evaluation that changes with each teacher. Collaborative scoring is a process that makes clear that if the college-educated adults in the school do not agree on what the word *proficient* means, how can a fourth grader figure it out? We caution that collaborative scoring requires some vulnerability—teachers do not like to have their work second-guessed by others. Therefore, when there is disagreement about how to score a piece of student work—and there will always be disagreements—the byword must be "the enemy is never each other—the enemy is ambiguity."

One way to frame the discussion about the connection between shared commitments and expectations is by developing a two-column "if-then" chart, such as the one in figure 2.1.

If we . . .	Then we . . .
Value a guaranteed and viable curriculum	Will have high expectations for teaching to the agreed-on curriculum and provide evidence students have learned the essential outcomes
Value assessing student progress in a frequent and timely manner	Will have high expectations for the collaborative development and use of common formative assessments
Value our commitment to the belief that students learn at different rates and in different ways	Will have high expectations for students to receive additional time, support and extension for their learning
Value a commitment to collaboration and working together	Will have high expectations for everyone being a contributing member of a collaborative team
Value a commitment to continuous improvement	Will have high expectations for attaining both short-term and long-term goals

FIGURE 2.1: If-then chart.

Caring enough to have high expectations involves committing to avoiding certain behaviors and attitudes. In their groundbreaking research on teacher expectations and student learning, Thomas L. Good and Jere E. Brophy (1990) point to twelve ways that some teachers treat students they have low expectations for differently.

1. Seating them farther from the teacher or seating them together in a group
2. Paying less attention to them in academic situations
3. Calling on them less often to answer classroom questions or to make public demonstrations
4. Providing less time for them to answer questions
5. Not staying with them in failure situations by providing fewer cues, asking fewer follow-up questions, and so on
6. Criticizing them more frequently than high-expectation students for incorrect responses
7. Praising them less frequently than high-expectation students for successful public responses
8. Praising them more frequently for marginal or inadequate public responses
9. Providing them with less accurate and detailed feedback
10. Failing to provide them with feedback about their responses as often
11. Demanding less work and effort from them
12. Interrupting their performance more frequently

In contrast, researchers Christine M. Rubie-Davies (2007, 2008) and Rubie-Davies and John Hattie (2024) find that teachers with high expectations spend more time teaching students, and they display many effective teaching behaviors such as carefully orienting students to the lesson, linking to prior knowledge, and carefully explaining concepts. Further, these teachers ask students a mix of open and closed questions, and, importantly, they ask high-level questions of all students, whereas teachers with low expectations most often ask closed questions and are dismissive of students who answer incorrectly. Finally, teachers with high expectations manage their classrooms far more positively than teachers with low expectations.

Research findings like these can be useful tools for team discussions on developing and committing to "stop doing" lists. Such collaboratively developed lists can demonstrate that the team cares enough to protect and safeguard their students from ineffective and often harmful practices (Reeves & Eaker, 2019).

Cultural caring requires more than gaining shared knowledge of behaviors that hinder student learning. Caring enough requires collaborative learning on best practices that have a strong research base, as well as practices proven effective by practitioners in their own classrooms through practitioner-driven action research.

There are multiple resources school leaders can use to find effective schooling practices. A few of the most highly recognized include the following.

- *Professional Learning Communities at Work and High Reliability Schools: Cultures of Continuous Learning* edited by Robert Eaker and Robert J. Marzano (2020)
- *Peak: How All of Us Can Achieve Extraordinary Things* by K. Anders Ericsson and Robert Pool (2017)
- *Visible Learning: A Synthesis of Over 800 Meta-Analyses Relating to Achievement* by John Hattie (2008)
- *Visible Learning: The Sequel* by John Hattie (2023)
- *What Effective Schools Do: Re-Envisioning the Correlates* by Lawrence W. Lezotte and Kathleen McKee Snyder (2011)
- *What Works in Schools: Translating Research into Action* by Robert J. Marzano (2003)
- *Classroom Instruction That Works: Research-Based Strategies for Increasing Student Achievement* by Robert J. Marzano, Jane E. Pollock, and Debra J. Pickering (2001)

The first step to any school-improvement effort is for educators to gain shared knowledge. If we want to increase student success because we care deeply for the students who are entrusted to us, then we, as a school community, must make a commitment to learn together. Student learning begins with adult learning.

Providing Individualized Time, Support, and Encouragement

It is an incontrovertible fact that students learn at different rates and in different ways. Yet, a primary principle of many, if not most schools, is that students must learn at the same rate, within the same amount of allotted time, and if they do not, they will receive negative feedback, usually in the form of bad grades.

Cultural caring requires a systematic plan to provide each student with additional time, support, and extension of learning, coupled with genuine and sincere encouragement (DuFour et al., 2024). The recurring message in a caring culture is, "We won't give up on you!" Larry Lezotte, the effective schools researcher, would frequently comment on the importance of a systematic plan to provide additional time and support for students who are experiencing difficulty with their learning. He emphasized that if you want to know whether a school has a culture of high expectations, see how the *school* responds *after students do not learn* (Lezotte, 1991).

What would evidence of high expectations and additional time, support, and extension of learning look like in a caring culture to an outside observer? DuFour and colleagues (2024) provide the following guidelines.

- Some students will need additional time and support to acquire the specific behaviors and dispositions they will need for success in school—and beyond.
- Create a master schedule that ensures all students have access to grade-level essential curricula and discontinue the practice of tracking.
- Create a master schedule where students receive additional time and support without missing core instruction.

- Systematic additional time and support should occur *within* the school day.
- Staff members work collaboratively to take *collective* responsibility for *each* student's success.
- The systematic plan for additional time and support must be designed in such a way that students receive additional time and support in a timely manner—as quickly as possible.
- The plan should be designed to target students for intervention by need. Staff are assigned based on who is best trained and has the experience and attitude to meet the specific needs of individual students. Students who are most at risk must have access to the most highly trained staff for their specific area of need.
- Students must be required to receive additional time and support; the additional support must not be optional.
- The intervention plan will also include provisions for additional time and support to extend and enrich the learning of students who have demonstrated proficiency.
- Being required to receive additional time and support should not be viewed as punishment—either by students or adults. Therefore, the plan for additional time and support will not deny students access to enrichment.
- Since some students will need additional time and opportunities to demonstrate mastery of essential curricula, the faculty should develop schoolwide grading practices that align with the intervention plan.
- The faculty will develop partnerships with parents to assist in student learning, but the plan for additional time and support must not be dependent on guardian participation.

We have frequently heard the excuse "I'd like to provide academic support, but the master schedule won't let me." Yet in the same district, other schools with the same funding, time constraints, and bargaining agreements are providing support during the school day. This is clearly a matter of will, not skill. There is also the matter of leadership courage, in which it will be necessary for leaders to say "This student needs support now—today—not after school and not next summer. If we do not address the academic support that this student needs, then they will simply stop coming to school." Situations like this are not merely a problem for the current school year, but a problem for decades of poverty, unemployment, and excessive use of the medical care and criminal justice systems (Ressa & Andrews, 2022). And who will pay for those decades of cost? The very people who oppose academic support and claim that "the master schedule makes it impossible."

Ultimately, designing a plan for additional time, support, and extension depends on how much we care. The question facing every school is this: Do we care enough to collaboratively develop a plan to provide *every* student with additional time, support, and extension of their learning, within the school day, regardless of the teacher to whom they are assigned?

Committing to Deep Caring

Genuine caring requires deep listening, compassion, empathy, encouragement, and a plan for additional time, support, and extension of learning. But, more than this, deep caring requires touching the emotions of everyone—administrators, teachers, support staff, students, and their parents or guardians. Deeply embedding a caring culture requires fidelity to the ideal that every student and adult deserves to feel special and to feel that the entire school community cares for them. Can schools grow from a mindset of measuring success almost exclusively by high-stakes state test results to *touching the emotional lives* of all stakeholders (Chapman & Sisodia, 2015)?

Deep caring requires that educators look for a higher, more meaningful standard of care. In her role as superintendent, Keating expected policies, practices, decision making, and every interaction to be measured though the lens of the question, "Would this be good enough for our own children?" We believe this is the challenge for all schools that seek to develop and embrace a caring culture: Do we care enough to create for all students the kind of caring culture we would want for our own children? And do we care enough to create a school that cares enough that educators would flock to teach in such a school?

Questions for Discussion

This chapter broadened the discussion of motivation to detail the work of the individual classroom teacher to promote care and support. Use the "Caring Classrooms Questions for Discussion" in the reproducible on page 36 to reflect on your school or district.

Caring Classrooms
Questions for Discussion

1. What does caring look like in your school? Consider not only classrooms but also hallways, lunchrooms, playgrounds, and other places where you can create a culture of caring.
2. We all believe that we have high expectations for students. What evidence could you share with colleagues and especially with people new to our profession that indicates those high expectations?
3. Reflect on your most recent staff meeting, department meeting, or collaborative team meeting. What are one or two changes that could improve the culture of respect and caring in those meetings?
4. In a single phrase or sentence, describe your "why." Why did you become an educator?

CHAPTER 3

Getting Feedback Right

I used to think giving more feedback and better feedback was the answer [to improving education], and it's the exact opposite.

— John Hattie

An essential element of a culture of caring is authenticity. When we care about people, we tell them the truth even when that is difficult to do. Caring parents tell their children, with unconditional love, when they fall short of expectations. Caring colleagues tell their peers when they can and must do better. Caring leaders say, with extraordinary kindness and compassion, that not everyone is meant to be a teacher, and offer to help those leaving teaching find a profession better suited for their gifts and desires. Being authentic means staying clear of providing destructive feedback and using ineffective measuring systems. Providing feedback that is fair, accurate, specific, and timely with reliability and validity is a cornerstone of a caring school culture. And instead of stopping with giving more and better feedback, as John Hattie (2023) notes in the opening quote, it is just as important to consider how teachers and students receive, interpret, and act on that feedback so they can use measurement to improve. Unfortunately, our culture has a long history of measurement gone wrong.

Measurement Gone Wrong

In the 19th century, practitioners of the pseudoscience phrenology claimed to be able to feel the bumps on people's heads and thereby assess their intelligence and personality traits. The 20th century brought more ill-fated attempts at measurement. The late Harvard professor Stephen Jay Gould (1996), in his book *The Mismeasure of Man*, writes that attempts in the 20th century to measure intelligence offered the illusion of precision without improving accuracy. Intelligence tests in the early 1900s were based on the needs of the military, as the United States prepared for the First World War, to assess who had the intelligence to become officers and who would be enlisted to serve under those officers. Gould (1996) argues that the results of these tests reflected ethnicity and income rather than intelligence. More than a century later, we persist in demonstrably inaccurate teacher and leadership evaluation systems that are more likely to reflect the zip code of the students and parental income than the quality of the teacher and leader (Stiggins, 2014).

In corporate America, a focus on short-term profits gives leaders an incentive to avoid long-term investments that may be in the best interests of shareholders, employees, and communities. Similarly, the incentives of teacher and leadership evaluations encourage short-term focusing on test scores rather than on long-term teacher and leadership quality. This helps us understand the difference between measurement and feedback. An Olympic judge can announce a score—let's say, a 7.5 for technical merit and 8.5 for artistic impression—but neither of those measurements helps the athlete improve. Constructive feedback, by contrast, helps the athlete, or student, understand how to get better, step by step, skill by skill. The key to feedback being constructive rather than a terminal judgment is the opportunity for the feedback to improve student performance. For example, rather than mark lab report results as wrong or an essay with only a score, constructive feedback identifies errors and provides the opportunity for students to improve their work and thus their learning by recalculating their results with a correct formula or providing more detail or expanding a conclusion in a written assignment. With this approach, students learn the material, as well as show respect for their teacher's feedback. Stanford psychologist David Yaeger (2024) notes that such "wise feedback," feedback given by teachers because they know students can improve their work, doubled the number of middle school students who resubmitted work.

Destructive Feedback

Some may think that destructive feedback is relentlessly critical, embarrassing the recipient and challenging the professionalism and competence of the students, teachers, or administrators receiving the feedback. It turns out that this is not the worst feedback; even worse is no feedback at all, or feedback that is contradictory, leaving the recipient bewildered. This situation is reminiscent of the tale "Three Blind Men and the Elephant," a parable from ancient Chinese and Buddhist texts (Baldwin, n.d.). The message is remarkably consistent across cultures and borders.

Three blind men come upon an elephant and one, touching its side, confidently announces that it is a wall. The second touches the trunk and fears that it is a snake. The third finds the ear and believes it to be a fan. We can apply this analogy to classroom observations. The first observer inspects the lesson plan and finds that it includes state standards and a minute-by-minute plan for the day. The second observer watches the delivery of instruction that clearly demonstrates the teacher's command of the subject. The third observer watches for the teacher's checks for understanding and direct engagement and reaction of students who are not focused on the lesson at hand. None of these observations are wrong, but when the three observers disagree, it can leave the teacher baffled. In every class, it's possible to excel in the eyes of one observer and fail in the eyes of another.

This same conflicting assessment of performance can happen with students. Many writing rubrics, for example, are excessively complex and unusable by students. By contrast, we have been in third-grade classrooms where a writing rubric was laminated to the students' desks and confident eight-year-olds could explain to us, "I only got a 2, but if I fix this sentence and have a better conclusion, I know I can get a 3."

In a culture of caring, there is no place for destructive feedback. That does not mean that feedback is always positive; positive feedback is encouraging, but it does not provide information students and adults need to improve. In a caring culture, leaders provide feedback to students, teachers, parents, and other leaders that is fair, accurate, specific, and timely. As educators, we should know what great feedback looks and feels like and what destructive feedback looks and feels like.

Destructive feedback is binary: The student's response is either right or wrong. After expressing a wrong answer, the student knows that they are wrong, but they have no clue about how to improve. Contrast this to the music teacher who, after hearing a mistaken note, coaches the student by indicating higher, lower, louder, softer, faster, or slower. Within seconds, the student can use that feedback to improve. That is what great teachers do—provide feedback so students can improve, minute by minute.

Authentic Feedback

In our work as consultants, we have asked audiences around the globe what they have found to be the characteristics of the most effective feedback they have ever received. Their answers are remarkably consistent. An easy way to recall these four qualities of effective feedback is the acronym FAST: fair, accurate, specific, and timely (Reeves, 2023).

Fair

First, recipients want feedback that is fair. That is, the same performance receives the same feedback. The nature of the feedback depends not on the appearance, age, or experience of the person to whom feedback is directed, but on their performance.

Accurate

Second, recipients want feedback that is accurate. That is, evaluators assess what the recipient thinks they are being assessed on. If, for example, educators are assessing effective checks for understanding, teachers should use equity sticks or random calling so that every student has an equal opportunity to participate rather than distort the observation by only calling on students whose hands are raised and knew the right answer before the class began. If we're assessing how an administrator or department head leads a faculty meeting or collaborative team in a PLC, we would expect to see 100 percent participation and vigorous and respectful debate about how to give students quality feedback. If we are assessing how a superintendent leads a cabinet meeting, we would provide feedback on how effectively they used time, how they encouraged deliberation and inquiry in the meeting, and how they draw out ideas from reluctant participants and challenge others who hog the microphone with orations.

Specific

Third, recipients expect feedback to be specific. The fundamental purpose of feedback, from the classroom to the boardroom, is to provide discussion that leads to improved performance. Vague instructions to "be more engaging" or "be less judgmental" do not help our colleagues who need to know precisely how to accomplish those goals.

We have asked principals who claim to be instructional leaders what the elements of effective instruction are and received the astonishing response, "Well, I know it when I see it." The educators and administrators we have interviewed frequently stress that feedback does not need to be positive—it just needs to be truthful; they need to have feedback that allows them to improve. Real self-esteem comes not from meaningless affirmation but rather from specific strategies to improve performance. When leaders provide such feedback, they model caring and the actions teachers must take with students. Ambiguous feedback, along with feedback that assumes that problems with student achievement and behavior are because the student is unmotivated and defiant, fails the standard of specificity.

Timely

Fourth, feedback must be timely. For an example of timely feedback, observe a music teacher. It doesn't make any difference if it's a class of fourth graders squeaking through their first violin practice or the show choir performing at a high school. What all great music teachers have in common is that they provide feedback that is immediate and precise. In the course of a fifteen-minute observation, you will see students learning, growing, and becoming more confident in their expertise. During a rehearsal, for example, a teacher directing an orchestra will tell the violin section to use a smaller bow stroke when playing eighth notes if the tempo is slowing down too much. A high school mathematics teacher might apply the principle of timely feedback by having students get up from their desks and solve problems on whiteboards and chart paper. Rather than traditional homework, students do real work in the classroom, with immediate feedback from their peers and the teacher. If they make a mistake, students can remedy the error immediately and, just as music students do, leave the class knowing that they know more than when they walked in the room.

Consider applying these criteria not just to how teachers provide feedback to students but also how the adults in your school receive feedback. Teachers and administrators typically receive feedback that fails to meet the criteria of fair, accurate, specific, and timely. Teachers receive an evaluation at the end of the year that includes critical comments about performance that occurred eight months earlier. It is worse for administrators; research suggests that the higher the administrative rank, the more ambiguous and less frequent the evaluation (Reeves, 2009).

Student Self-Assessment

Creating a culture of caring is not about false affirmations to make students feel good. Rather, genuine caring requires empowering students to give themselves feedback by accurately assessing their work and creating a road map for improvement. One great way to accelerate this process, which we have seen used from primary grades to graduate students, uses a three-column rubric with the following headings.

1. **Left column:** Explicit expectations (in student accessible language)
2. **Middle column**: Student self-assessment
3. **Right column:** Teacher comments (only when the teacher disagrees with the student self-assessment)

Most rubrics are designed for use by teachers and other evaluators. The student submits the work, the teacher grades it, and that's usually the end of the process. In the three-column rubric, by contrast, students take responsibility for assessing their own work and the teachers can focus on those areas where the students are unclear about whether or not they are proficient. The teacher feedback is not the final evaluation, but rather a method of improving student work in response to that feedback. These rubrics can be used for any grade level. Primary students might have simple *I can . . .* statements, while secondary students can have more elaborate multilevel rubrics. The key is that the language of the rubrics must be accessible to students.

The three-column rubric engages student interest because students take on the powerful role of assessor. Teachers no longer have to write comments or provide rubric scores for every part of an assessment. They can save time by focusing exclusively on student misunderstandings. Teachers who use this technique report that the time devoted to evaluating student work has declined by more than 60 percent (Reeves, 2020a). This not only saves teachers time, it also gives students feedback much more quickly.

For example, an intermediate mathematics class is assigned the following problem:

Look at the data set that shows the United States' gross domestic product (GDP) from 1928 to 1938. Plot the points on a graph, label the axes, and explain the formula that includes the y-intercept and slope. Make a prediction about what the data on the y axis would look like if you extended the graph from 1938 to 1943. Explain your prediction based on what you know about events from 1938 to 1943.

Figure 3.1 (page 44) shows a three-column rubric sample.

My Work	Student Self-Assessment	Teacher Assessment
1. I correctly plotted the points from the data table on the graph.	I plotted the GDP on the y axis and the years on the *x* axis.	✓
2. I correctly labeled the *x* and *y* axes on the graph.	I labeled the *x* and *y* axes.	Please label not only GDP and year but also the units on the *x* and *y* axes.
3. I wrote the formula for the graph using the $y = mx + b$ formulation and explained the formula in words.	The line connecting the dots is not perfectly straight, but I connected them the best I could. I showed the *y*-intercept and the slope of the line.	✓
4. I made a prediction about what the graph would look like if the *x* axis was extended to the right by ten years.	I copied the first draft onto another paper, with the *x* axis having five more years.	Please elaborate on your explanation. What happened from 1938 to 1943 that might influence your prediction? Try to find the real *y* axis data for those years and see how it compares to your prediction.

FIGURE 3.1: Sample three-column rubric for an intermediate mathematics problem.

In another example, consider the following middle school social studies question:

Look at three maps of the United States, one from 1800, one from 1830, and one from 1860. Why did the maps change and what was the impact on the United States?

Figure 3.2 shows a three-column rubric sample.

This technique will dramatically reduce the time it takes to grade papers and, more importantly, improve the sense of competence and confidence by students who know that they can assess their own work with accuracy and consistency. Moreover, self-assessment is a key skill in college and the world of work.

My Work	Student Self-Assessment	Teacher Assessment
1. I accurately described the changes in each map, including new states and territories.	I made a three-column chart for 1800, 1830, and 1860 showing states and territories.	✓
2. I explained the reasons for changes in the maps.	I showed the laws that approved expansion.	Please expand your explanation to include actions that were not authorized, wars, and executive actions.
3. I explained at least two controversies about westward expansion.	I wrote a story about the Trail of Tears and summarized a debate on the Mexican-American War.	✓
4. I explained the impact of westward expansion on Indigenous nations.	I made a table showing the number of members of Indigenous nations who were killed and who died of disease.	Please expand your answer to include the loss of property and economic opportunity and the long-term consequences of displacement.

FIGURE 3.2: Sample three-column rubric for a middle school social studies task.

The Need for Reliability and Validity

The basic requirements for any assessment, from a first-grade reading test to the evaluation of veteran teachers and administrators, are reliability and validity. *Reliability* is a measure of consistency. If you go to the grocery store and put a pound of bananas on the scale and it reads sixteen ounces, and then a minute later the same bunch of bananas weighs in at twenty-four ounces, and the next minute, the scale shows eight ounces, we will not exclaim, "What a remarkable bunch of bananas!" Rather, we would conclude that the scale was broken. Similarly, when the same teacher is rated an A one year and then, within the same school and using the same teaching practices and the same curriculum, is rated a D the next year, we should not conclude that the teacher is incompetent, but rather that the scale—the teacher assessment—is broken.

Though it has been widely discredited, many states continue to use—sometimes as a result of legislative mandate—value-added assessment. The original research for this system was conducted in Tennessee in the 1980s and 1990s and showed that some teachers added value over the course of three years and other teachers did not (Stiggins, 2014). But there were two deep flaws in the system. First, it assumed that there were stable student populations, an assumption not warranted, especially in high-poverty schools. Second, the variance-covariance matrixes on which the value-added model depended were full of missing values. Rather than admit that the data were missing, the model inserted estimated values based on a formula that, among other things, included the free- and reduced-lunch status of the student.

The second essential requirement for any assessment is *validity*—that is, we are assessing what we intend to assess. While there is widespread discontent with mathematics scores (Jimenez, 2023; Mineo, 2024; Yu, 2024), few people have asked this essential question: What are we really assessing? The labels of assessments bear the title of "mathematics," however, a more accurate label would be "English language literacy with numbers." If you serve a significant number of English learners—and their ranks are growing every year (Najarro, 2024)—ask your mathematics teachers to do the following simple experiment.

Create a simple ten-item mathematics assessment. Five items have only numbers, symbols, and letters appropriate for the grade level. The next five items have the same mathematical challenges embedded in a story problem. Then compare the numbers and symbols-only results with the story problem results. If the scores are higher in the former category compared to the latter, it suggests that your student scores are heavily influenced by students' English proficiency.

The same validity issue occurs in teacher and leadership evaluations. Given the document-heavy evaluation systems in place across the United States, we must ask, "Are we evaluating the effectiveness of teaching and leadership practices or are we evaluating a stack of papers?" In some states, the last month of the school year is devoted not to teaching and leadership, but to building portfolios to defend a high rating on the evaluation system. Every one of these hours devoted to the document drill of prevailing teacher and leadership evaluation systems is an hour not devoted to teaching, learning, and leadership.

Marshall's Observation Tools

Valid assessments depend on linking actual observations, from the third-grade classroom to the superintendent's cabinet meetings, to clearly established criteria. For teacher evaluation, the state of the art is free and open source. Created by Kim Marshall, editor of the widely influential *Marshall Memo* (MarshallMemo.com), the system relies on frequent and unannounced very short observations. Marshall's (2024) observation tools get to the essence of effective instruction so that observers can provide support throughout the year for improved practices in instructional delivery, classroom management, student engagement, and other critical areas. Best of all, Marshall's observation tools provide a road map for teachers to get to the next level of effectiveness. Unlike the vast majority of teacher observation tools used in schools and sometimes mandated by state officials, Marshall's system does not depend on voluminous documentation. The observer can simply highlight what they see and not highlight what they don't see. Very little writing is required; the document speaks for itself. Most importantly, Marshall's observation tool provides an essential ingredient of fairness: The same performance receives the same score. Many districts and states have made six- and seven-figure investments in teacher evaluation instruments that are not nearly as effective as those Marshall provides for free. Figure 3.3 (page 48) shows an example of Marshall's (2024) observation tool for delivery of instruction.

	Highly Effective	Effective	Improvement Necessary	Does Not Meet Standards
	The teacher . . .			
Expectations	Exudes high expectations, urgency, and determination that all students will master the material.	Conveys to students: This is important, you can do it, and I'm not going to give up on you.	Tells students that the subject matter is important and they need to work hard.	Gives up on some students as hopeless.
Mindset	Actively inculcates a growth mindset: Takes risks, learns from mistakes, and believes that through effective effort students can and will achieve at high levels.	Teaches students that effective effort, not innate ability, is the key.	Doesn't counteract students' belief that innate ability is what makes the difference.	Communicates a fixed mindset about ability: Some students have it, and some don't.
Framing	Highlights lesson goals and unit essential questions up front and has students summarize and internalize key learning at the end.	Highlights lesson goals at the beginning of the lesson and has students sum up what they've learned at the conclusion.	Tells students the main learning objectives of each lesson but doesn't wrap things up at the end.	Begins and ends lessons without giving students a sense of what it's all about.
Connections	Engages students in each unit's and lesson's content and vocabulary by activating their interests and prior knowledge.	Links newly introduced lesson content and vocabulary to students' interests and prior knowledge.	Is only sometimes successful in making the subject interesting and relating it to things students already know.	Rarely hooks students' interests or makes connections to their lives.
Clarity	Presents material clearly and explicitly, with well-chosen examples and vivid, appropriate language.	Uses clear explanations, appropriate language, and examples to present material.	Sometimes uses language and explanations that are fuzzy, confusing, or inappropriate.	Often presents material in a confusing way and/or uses language that is inappropriate.

Repertoire	Uses a wide range of well-chosen, effective strategies, questions, materials, technology, and groupings to accelerate student learning.	Orchestrates effective strategies, questions, materials, technology, and groupings to foster student learning.	Uses a limited range of classroom strategies, questions, materials, and groupings with mixed success.	Uses only one or two teaching strategies and types of materials and fails to reach most students.
Engagement	Gets virtually all students involved in focused activities, actively learning and problem-solving, losing themselves in the work.	Has students actively think about, discuss, and use the ideas and skills being taught.	Attempts to get students actively involved, but some students are disengaged.	Mostly lectures to passive students or has them plod through textbooks and worksheets.
Differentiation	Successfully reaches virtually all students by skillfully differentiating and scaffolding and using peer and adult helpers.	Scaffolds instruction and uses peer and adult helpers to accommodate most students' learning needs.	Attempts to accommodate lessons for students with learning needs, but with mixed success.	Fails to differentiate instruction for students with learning needs.
Nimbleness	Deftly adapts lessons and units to exploit teachable moments and correct misunderstandings.	Is flexible about modifying lessons to take advantage of teachable moments.	Sometimes doesn't take advantage of teachable moments.	Is rigid and inflexible with lesson plans and rarely takes advantage of teachable moments.
Overall rating: **Comments:**				

Source: Marshall, 2024, p. 4. Reprinted with permission.

FIGURE 3.3: Marshall's delivery of instruction rubric.

The Leadership Performance Matrix

For leadership assessment, Reeves (2009) offers the Leadership Performance Matrix, based on a study of leadership evaluations in thirty-seven states. It is free and open source and is remarkably different from other prevailing leadership assessments. It provides ten dimensions of leadership, each with a detailed four-level rubric so that leaders can have a clear road map for progress, just as Marshall's observation tool provides a road map for improvement in teaching practice.

1. **Resilience:** The leader acknowledges mistakes and helps the entire system learn from those mistakes.
2. **Personal behavior and professional ethics:** There is no deviation from standards of professional conduct.
3. **Student achievement:** This is not only a matter of state test scores but also a holistic description of how students are learning and growing in their academic achievement.
4. **Decision making:** The leader actively seeks alternative decisions and has clear criteria for how to make decisions so that decisions are transparent and openly considered by all stakeholders.
5. **Communication:** The leader communicates effectively with staff and community and, where appropriate, in multiple languages.
6. **Faculty development:** The leader provides professional learning differentiated for those new to the profession and the seasoned veterans.
7. **Leadership development:** The leader prepares an effective bench of future leaders that will serve the school and the entire educational system.
8. **Time, task, and project management:** The leader has a clearly established, prioritized task list and shares this information with the staff.
9. **Technology:** The leader uses technology effectively without being consumed by it.

10. **Personal professional learning:** The leader demonstrates lifelong learning, consistently upgrading leadership skills and knowledge.

There are two other factors that make the Leadership Performance Matrix valuable for school leaders. First, it focuses on resilience, the willingness of the leader to admit mistakes, learn from them, and at the highest level, help the entire system learn from them. Second, nobody gets a perfect score. This is a hard pill to swallow for leaders who have received perfect evaluations throughout their career. But the fact is that nobody is perfect in all ten dimensions of leadership. The honest conversation between leaders and their governing boards or supervisors must sound like this:

> I know my strengths and weaknesses. I'm really good at instructional leadership, leadership and faculty development, and community communication. But I'm going to need a complementary team that has different strengths in data analysis and other areas. I'm not pretending to be the perfect leader, but I will develop an exemplary team that, together, is strong in every area.

A culture of caring requires leaders who are willing to be vulnerable. An essential element of vulnerability is acknowledging error. In a culture of caring, leaders know that they can only help others when they are willing to be vulnerable and admit mistakes first.

Questions for Discussion

This chapter introduced the importance of feedback to sustain a committed and caring environment and describes authentic feedback, including two tools for leaders to use. Use the "Getting Feedback Right Questions for Discussion" in the reproducible on page 52 to reflect on your school or district.

Getting Feedback Right
Questions for Discussion

1. Before your next meeting, agree to observe—just for fifteen or twenty minutes—an athletic practice or music practice. Plan to share what you noticed and how the best coaches and music directors can inform classroom feedback practices in every subject and grade level.
2. Think of the best feedback you have received, whether as a professional, a student, or for work outside of education. Share with your colleagues the characteristics of that feedback.
3. What are the ways, other than grades, test scores, and marks on student work, that you can give students effective feedback?
4. Reliability—consistency of scoring—is essential for every assessment. How do you know that your assessments of student and adults are reliable?
5. Validity—assessing what you intend to assess—is the other essential requirement for every assessment. How do you know that your assessments of students and adults are valid?

CHAPTER 4

Supporting Caring Beyond the Classroom

Encouraging a child means that one or more of the following critical life messages are coming through, either by word or by action. I believe in you, I trust you, I know you can handle this, you are listened to, you are cared for, you are very important to me.

—Barbara Coloroso

Not every parent or guardian is able to provide the same quality of support to their children. In the book *Thirty Million Words: Building a Child's Brain* (Suskind, 2015), researchers Dana Suskind, Beth Suskind, and Leslie Lewinter-Suskind document the stark disadvantage from birth to age five that children born into low-income families experience. This disadvantage stems from the lack of books in the home and, especially, from the lack of conversations with adults, many of whom are working long hours in low-paying jobs to support their family. Yet there is one quality that is essentially equal, and that is the unconditional love that parents offer to their children.

In his excellent book *How the Other Half Learns: Equality, Excellence, and the Battle Over School Choice*, Robert Pondiscio (2019) provides compelling evidence that parents in New York City's high-poverty schools are vital to propelling their children to achievement that rivals the wealthy suburbs. In this chapter, we explore how parents, as their children's first teachers, can have a profoundly positive impact on students if, and only if, educators and school administrators give those parents the welcome and respect that they deserve.

Making Safety the Top Priority

Most parents remember well the first time their child rode a bike around the block. In the seconds after they slipped out of sight, those parents' hearts leaped into their throats, wondering if they qualified for the Worst Parent in the World Award. Miraculously, their child made it around the block, beaming with confidence. Nevertheless, the anxiety and tension surrounding that first trip around the block persisted as their child went to school. Before Doug's son Brooks went to kindergarten, they made regular trips to the local school playground so he was accustomed to the space. When the first day of kindergarten came, Brooks was happy to bid farewell while other children were sobbing and clinging to parents. And let's be clear—parents, including Doug, were crying too.

In the 21st century, parental concerns about safety are amplified by the news of school shootings, despite the fact that students are at higher risk being driven to school compared to being in a school shooting. We all identify with the terror of not knowing if our children are safe. Caring leaders do not lecture parents about statistical probabilities; rather, they have consistent and clear conversations about how they will keep their children safe. As this book goes to press, a school administrator in Iowa died to give students time to escape a shooter. In other tragic shootings, teachers have sacrificed themselves to save the lives of students. While news of these events may lead parents to focus on shootings and threats to physical safety, we are also concerned about the psychological safety of our children.

Harvard Medical School psychologist Ellen Braaten (2023) has studied children exposed to traumatic events from the global pandemic to natural disasters to the terrorist attacks of September 11, 2001. She concludes that children need to know the answers to three questions:

1. Am I safe?
2. Are the people I love safe?
3. How will these events affect me in the future?

Braaten reminds us that children may need many reassurances about their safety and the safety of the people they love. During the school closures associated with the pandemic, many students were left home alone while their parents worked essential jobs—in hospitals and retail stores, or as delivery drivers, garbage collectors, scientists, and healthcare workers. Those children were without essential parent assurance when they most needed it. While more than five years after the onset of the pandemic in March of 2020, it is too early to completely understand the full effects of the pandemic, but some facts are undeniable. Many students suffered significant learning loss, as very limited virtual school—sometimes one hour a day and sometimes nothing at all—led to months of learning loss. In high-poverty schools where students were struggling before COVID, the learning loss was even greater (World Bank Group, 2021). In our work with teachers around the United States, two other factors in the post-COVID world continue to distract teachers and school leaders: chronic absenteeism and a spike in student misbehavior.

Schools have had several consistent reactions to the challenges of low academic performance, absenteeism, and behavioral challenges. In response to learning loss, have schools radically transformed their schedules to give teachers and students the time they need to improve essential reading and mathematics skills? The answer, unfortunately, is no. We ask every audience we address in our consulting work how today's schedule and time allocation are different than they were before the pandemic. More than 90 percent of educators say that there is no change. The vast majority continue discredited grading practices, such as the use of averaging—a certain way to diminish the hope and resilience of students—and punishing students for missing homework. Every spring, we overhear comments such as, "There's no way this student can pass—he's dug a hole too deep." We should not wonder why these students stop turning in any work and, for that matter, stop coming to school.

There are wonderful exceptions, with academic interventions and tutoring occurring during the school day and effective practice (as opposed to the futile practice of homework) happening in class. Other schools are increasing attendance and achievement by boldly embracing teaching, assessment, and leadership practices that work. A growing number of schools are embracing collaborative problem solving (Ablon, 2018) to develop constructive ways to first understand the roots of misbehavior and then, with students' involvement, develop thoughtful and constructive ways to give students the tools they need for self-regulation.

Assuming Positive Motives

If you have been confronted with a parent, teacher, or educational leader facing a sullen, angry, defiant, and disengaged student, we know it is not always easy to assume positive motives. "Why can't they be like we were?" we wonder. Perhaps they can be the perfectly behaved child that we recall in the rearview mirror. But as psychologist J. Stuart Ablon (2018) argues, poor behavior is rarely the result of a lack of will, but rather a lack of skill. Most disciplinary regimes, he argues, are eerily similar to the behavior modification practices that he has observed in prisons and mental hospitals. And who almost never participates in developing these discipline programs? The students. We assume that we know what motivates students—grades and recognition—when it's entirely possible that we are using 20th century motivational techniques on 21st century students.

In her masterful book *Smart Kids Who Couldn't Care Less*, Braaten (2023) notes from her therapeutic practice that in family counseling sessions, parents complain that they are ready to give up. "I just don't know how to motivate them! And they are addicted to video games! They just don't seem to care." Yet Braaten observes that very few of the students who come to athletic or musical practice sessions had learning disabilities or other diagnosable conditions. The condition of "not caring" cannot be fixed with drugs or curriculum; rather, it requires that the adults in the children's lives take seriously their responsibility to identify the root causes of their demotivation. Parents and teachers are eager to have students set goals—the system that worked for them as successful adults (Braaten, 2023).

Let us place ourselves in the position of the student. We hear anything but positive feedback as criticism, belittling, and a personal attack. As discussed earlier, adults are clear on what they want: feedback that is fair, accurate, specific, and timely—FAST (Reeves, 2009). Ask students how feedback from parents and teachers appears to them. They might come up with another acronym: false, accusatory, intimidating, and lethal—FAIL. This sort of fear is the enemy of learning, as Harvard professor Amy Edmondson (2018) argues in her brilliant research on hospital settings. She notes that a fearful environment where mistakes are covered up is literally a matter of life and death. When people are afraid to challenge the mistakes of surgeons, pilots, and chemical company executives, people die. Reeves (2021b) adapted this research in hospitals to the world of education in *Fearless Schools: Building Trust, Resilience, and Psychological Safety.*

Before we start judging students and colleagues about their lack of motivation, consider our perspective if, as Ablon (2023) suggests, we assume good will, that they want to do well, and need incremental opportunities to develop the skills to do so. If we begin with the assumption that students and colleagues could be good but just won't, we are the unstoppable force running into an immovable object. But if we begin with the assumption of good motives—that students and colleagues want to do well—we have opened the door for productive dialogue and the opportunity to celebrate small wins. At the very heart of a culture of caring is assuming positive intent by those with whom we might be tempted to clash.

The assumption of good will is as important for adults as for students. We have heard many educators and administrators complain that "parents just don't value education." We've heard administrators complain about poor teacher quality while they continue to provide year after year of ineffective evaluations to effective teachers. The converse is true, with teachers complaining about ineffective administrators and taking votes of no confidence but rarely providing constructive feedback on specifically how leaders can improve. That condition is related to the revolving door of principals and superintendents, particularly in high-poverty schools and districts, and school board members who regularly face abuse and insults.

Imagine a conversation in which we all assume good will and good motives by the students and adults we encounter. Then our disagreements would not be about their deficient character or emotional and intellectual weaknesses, but rather about how we find common ground on values, on our love for kids, and respect for one another. We must resist being pulled into (or creating) a toxic environment in which people who disagree with us are made out to be villains. We can do better.

Encouraging Delayed Gratification

One of the most important skills that children learn is the value of delayed gratification. This is a rare quality in many schools and families since parents and teachers may interpret the word *caring* as avoiding stress and anxiety for children. The truth is, as Stanford Psychologist Kelly McGonigal (2015) and New York University psychologist Wendy Suzuki (2021) demonstrate, the demand for immediate gratification and the avoidance of stress and anxiety not only harm students as they proceed to higher levels of education but also harm their mental health. We understand that there are toxic levels of stress and anxiety that can be paralyzing and debilitating, but the evidence from McGonigal (2015) and Suzuki (2021) strongly suggests that when students are protected from all stress and anxiety, even small inconveniences, it can lead to a meltdown. Sometimes the impetus for immediate gratification is driven by the politicians and, too often, school administrators, who insist that students are customers. They are not. Customers get immediate gratification, returning products they do not like and complaining to professors and employers that any error is not the fault of the student or customer but rather the fault of a bad teacher and toxic boss. Students are not, however, customers; they are students, and students thrive on delayed gratification, provided that teachers and parents get it right.

Importantly, parents play a role in helping students learn the importance of delayed gratification. Not all parents understand why this is so important and how they can help. Parent meetings can be devoted to discussions about the importance of students learning about delayed gratification. Individual parent-teacher conferences can also play an important role.

Parents hire tutors and negotiate with teachers for higher grades. Well-meaning teachers routinely give high marks to student work that is far below the standards the school has set. One of the ideas in the work of Bob Eaker and the late Richard DuFour is the essential need for teachers to agree on what the word *proficient* means. Coming to such an agreement means that a collaborative team of teachers looks at a piece of student work and compares it to the expectations of the scoring guide or checklist. This is not an easy process, but when collaborative teams persist, they get better and better—that is, they move from angry disagreements to a 92 percent level of agreement (Reeves, 2023). It is not perfect, but it is far better than when everyone was, in DuFour's words, engaged in "private practice" (DuFour, DuFour, Eaker, & Many, 2006). Reeves (2023) researched the operations of teacher teams who engaged in collaborative scoring and found that not only did the quality of their scoring improve, it also dramatically saved time. With each iteration of collaborative scoring, disagreements ended not with arguments but rather with the reminder of the adage, "The enemy is not each other—the enemy is ambiguity." Each disagreement led not to an argument about the student's work, but rather a collaborative effort to improve the precision and clarity of the scoring guide or checklist.

From a student's perspective, this process meant that a low mark was not a badge of shame but a clearly outlined opportunity to move to the next level. For as much as adults complain about video games, the language of "getting to the next level" is precisely what students say just after they have been obliterated by an alien spaceship in a video game. There is an ethic of constant improvement and the use of feedback, including failure, as a fuel for learning.

When students are deeply engaged in something important to them, whether it is playing a game or writing the fourth draft of an article for the school newspaper, they are learning the value of delayed gratification. This flies in the face of the often-heard assertion that students must get it right the first time. That ethic is the enemy of learning and only encourages cheating, the use of artificial intelligence and, most commonly, inappropriate levels of parent support. Examples of things teachers should not do include withholding encouragement, expecting students to complete homework within an unreasonable time frame or when they are too tired, providing students with misinformation when parents do not understand the assignments, and so on. The key to delayed gratification is the immediate opportunity to apply feedback to improve. By *immediately*, we do not mean the next round of state tests, but time that is measured in seconds.

Every family is different, and each has its own unique strengths and challenges. While parental partnerships with teachers are important, each family's needs, as well as their responses, differ from family to family. There is no one program or initiative that will be 100 percent effective with every family and their children. There is only so much that schools and individual teachers can do to assist parents, but there are things schools and teachers can do to help. First, in every interaction—every conversation—teachers should make it clear to parents that they should feel free to ask for help. Perhaps a parent does not understand how to help their child with a homework assignment, or perhaps the child has given their parents information that the parents doesn't understand. The important point is that parents know the teacher cares about their child and the child's learning and wants to help in any way they can.

Second, schools can offer workshops, programs, and other resources to teach parents ways to help their child. For example, the language and processes of mathematics might be different from what students' parents learned in school. Workshops on how to help students with their homework can be valuable, as can workshops on other topics. Remember, the PLC at Work process is about enhancing the learning of everyone—including parents.

Many schools provide a homework hotline—a telephone number parents can call during specified times to ask questions about homework problems with which they are struggling. Perhaps most importantly, in all interactions with parents, all school personnel should model interest and caring in each parent's children.

In a culture of caring, students learn not to rely on teachers, parents, or other external forces to create high expectations. Rather, students themselves learn to understand what great performance looks like and what they should do to challenge themselves to make daily progress toward their goals. How quickly students learn this differs from individual to individual, but learning to take responsibility for their own learning is a consistent goal for all students in a culture of caring.

Questions for Discussion

This chapter addressed the need for student support beyond the school walls and how teachers can help by assuming positive motivations from students and parents and encouraging skills such as delayed gratification to support students beyond the classroom. Use the "Supporting Caring Beyond the Classroom Questions for Discussion" in the reproducible on page 62 to reflect on your school or district.

Supporting Caring Beyond the Classroom Questions for Discussion

1. What are your own experiences with delayed gratification? What were your frustrations? How can you use your personal experiences with delayed gratification to communicate with students and parents?
2. What in your experience are parents' greatest frustrations with schools and teachers? What were your most successful experiences in dealing with those frustrations?
3. What are the barriers to creating more constructive relationships with parents and students? What are the opportunities for creating great relationships with parents and students in your school?

CHAPTER 5

Caring and Teacher Needs

Why can't our kids do as well as students in China, Singapore, and Korea?

Because in China, Singapore, and Korea, teachers are treated with respect by students, parents, and citizens.

—Douglas Reeves

When done right, being a teacher is hard work. For teachers to do their work right, school leaders must fulfill teachers' needs. When asked what they need, teachers respond similarly to other professionals: They want respect, appropriate pay, a safe environment, resources, and a supportive and caring environment. The structural needs, like appropriate pay, safety, and resources, are typically a matter of political decisions made by states and school boards. School leaders, however, can do their part to fulfill teachers' needs.

When thinking about cultural caring in schools and classrooms, our initial thoughts usually focus on creating caring cultures for students. After all, ensuring high levels of learning for all students to enable their future success is the core reason schools exist. However, cultural caring requires a much broader focus. Creating a true culture of caring requires caring for everyone within the school community and doing so with fidelity. In fact, when undertaking the journey to create a caring culture throughout the school community, the place to begin is with a focus on adults within the school—especially with teachers.

Teachers need and deserve leaders who are caring individuals. Teachers also need leaders who have the leadership skills and the desire to embed a caring culture throughout the school or school district.

Reframing What Teachers Need

Schools are complex organizations. Meeting the needs of teachers requires a conceptual framework, not only about how we as leaders view teachers, but also how teachers—and the act of teaching—can be viewed through multiple lenses.

One way to think about what teachers need is through the work that Lee Bolman and Terry Deal (2021) present in their book *Reframing Organizations*. Viewing teachers' needs and how they can be met through Bolman and Deal's "four frames" gives leaders a way of viewing teacher needs through four distinct, *interconnected*, perspectives. These four frames are (1) structural needs, (2) psychological and human needs, (3) political needs, and (4) symbolic needs. We discuss each of these frames in the following sections.

Structural Needs

Bolman and Deal's (2021) first frame is a structural perspective; namely, how the school and district are organized. The structural frame includes such organizational aspects as policies, resource allocation, organizational charts, job descriptions, time allocation, schedules, evaluation processes, staff hiring and development, goal setting, and accountability and evaluation processes, just to name a few.

A focus on teacher needs requires deep examination of all the major aspects of the school district and school structures. More specifically, in a caring culture, what do teachers need from a structural perspective? Topics that can form the foundation for discussion around teachers' *structural* needs include caring leaders; collaborative teaming; time; high-quality training; policies, procedures, and practices that support care; and appropriate and meaningful compensation. We address each of these in the following sections.

Caring Leaders

Developing a culture of caring cannot be successful without caring leaders. The need for strong, effective leadership is one of the central correlates of effective schools (Lezotte & Snyder, 2011). Even if there are many caring teachers in a school, without caring leaders the central tenants of caring behavior and attitudes cannot be brought together, developed, maintained, and embedded deeply into every classroom.

Teachers also need effective, caring leaders who *model* the behaviors that are expected of others, both students and adults. Caring leaders model *intentional connection* (Janks, 2024), which "fosters authentic relationships based on empathy, respect, and mutual understanding." Caring leaders send important messages to stakeholders outside the school, like parents, thus paving the way for positive interactions between teachers and parents and community members. How can leaders expect teachers to uphold a culture of care when they themselves do not do so as evidenced by their actions?

One of the most obvious ways leaders communicate that they care is by providing teachers with the resources, support, and encouragement they need to be successful. Richard Elmore (2004) refers to this responsibility as "reciprocal accountability." He describes the term as follows:

> Reciprocal accountability—For every increment of performance I demand of you, I have an equal responsibility to provide you with the capacity to meet that expectation. Likewise, for every investment you make in my skill and knowledge, I have a reciprocal responsibility to demonstrate some new increment in performance. (p. 93)

Cultural caring for teachers requires effective implementation of the reciprocal accountability concept, especially by leaders demonstrating they care enough to provide the necessary structural resources for teachers to succeed. And these structures leaders build go beyond what is needed inside school walls. For example, a school leader helped staff organize babysitting services for a newly single mother so she wouldn't lose much-needed income. Another leader donated his time to support teachers who organized a laundry service for students in need of freshly washed clothes.

Collaborative Teaming

Teaming refers to teams composed of teachers who teach the same or similar content. How teachers are organized within the school structure affects the degree to which they can effectively care for their students and each other. While there is no one right way to structure collaborative teams, if the central mission of schools is to demonstrate we care enough for our students to ensure high levels of learning, then teachers should be organized into teams based on their teaching the same or similar content. In a PLC, teams are most often made up of teachers from the same grade level or course. When a school is small or teachers are singletons—the only teacher of a course or subject, like music—teachers can organize in other ways so that collaboration is meaningful, such as in a vertical team with teachers in the grades or courses below and above theirs or with teachers in other schools or districts.

The structural needs of teachers go beyond simply organizing them into collaborative teams and include providing teachers with clarity regarding what teams are expected to do. Central to this is ensuring that teams take *collective responsibility* for student and team success. Working collaboratively with collective responsibility is the second big idea of a PLC (DuFour et al., 2024). In PLCs, educators work together to achieve common goals, for which members are mutually accountable. As DuFour and his colleagues (2024) maintain, "It is difficult to overstate the importance of collaborative teams in the improvement process" and collaboration "does not lead to improved results unless people are focused on the right work" (p. 19). This includes working together to build shared knowledge on the best way to achieve goals and meet the needs of students (DuFour et al., 2024). This is what professionals in any field are expected to do, "whether they are curing patients, winning lawsuits, or helping all students learn," DuFour and colleagues (2024) write, adding, "Members of a *professional* learning community are expected to work and learn together" (p. 19).

Without a focus on collaboration and collective responsibility, a teacher might ask, "Can't you just give me *my* students and leave me alone?" In a PLC, leadership's answer to this must be a consistent "No!" It is impossible to create a caring culture when teachers are left alone to act individually. Schooling has become so complex that even the very best teachers cannot successfully meet all the demands and needs required of them. Leaders must care enough to have high expectations for collective responsibility through collaborative teaming.

Time

No one would conclude that the demands on teachers are decreasing. Students are expected to learn more, at higher levels of rigor, and teachers are expected to meet this expectation within a culture of increasing accountability, with less public and political support, and *within less time*. A rarely discussed structural aspect of schooling is how the state and national political obsession with high-stakes testing has robbed teachers of time to teach and students of time to learn. Each spring, valuable instructional time is spent preparing for state assessments, followed by as much as a week devoted to testing.

Diminishing time to teach and learn has a direct effect on student (and teacher) success. Saphier and his coauthors (2008) write, "School effectiveness researchers over the past three decades have ranked time—and time related to instructional variables—either number one or number two on a list of eight to ten factors that are important to student achievement" (p. 50).

While protecting instructional time, particularly time for core instruction, is important, time for teams to collaborate is also essential. Collaboration time needs to be within the school day, respecting the fact that after school or before school, teachers have other responsibilities, particularly family responsibilities. Leaders who care make sure the school schedule addresses time (a minimum of one hour or class period per week) within the school day for team collaboration.

Sometimes the constraints on teacher time are self-imposed by schools, teachers, and advocacy groups. No one comes to the state capitol building to demand fewer standards or that teachers teach fewer subjects. In fact, the demands to expand the social studies curriculum in particular have increased without adding a single minute to the time available. The *1619 Project* (Hannah-Jones, 2021) is a perfect example, as schools rightfully want students to understand the origins of slavery on the North American continent and advocates of critical thinking want students to evaluate the claims made in that and other books. But what do teachers give up teaching? The Civil War? Economic calamities? The civil rights movement? The most common excuse we hear for minimum classroom discussion and maximum teacher lecturing is, "I have to cover it all," as if coverage were equal to learning. Some secondary schools have nine periods a day, giving each teacher fewer minutes for each class and leaving no time for academic support. Higher performing schools have fewer periods—no more than five or six—and do not succumb to the pressures of a cafeteria curriculum in which every local and state interest group demands that their curriculum priorities are crammed into the school day (Reeves, 2016, 2018).

Respecting and protecting teacher time, like most aspects of schooling, begins at the top with the superintendent and building-level principals. School leaders must understand what teachers need time to do, and provide a structure—a schedule—that provides more time for high-priority engagement between teachers and students, and between each other.

One way to think of teacher time is through two distinct lenses. The first is instructional time, and instructional time can be broken down into *allocated* time, which is the time teachers are allocated to teach, and *academic engaged* time, or the time students are actively engaged in learning. While teachers are generally allocated the same amount of time to teach, the amount of academic engaged time varies greatly, from teacher to teacher.

The second lens through which to view teacher time is the need for planning time. Teacher planning time is of two types: individual teacher planning time, which includes grading papers and so forth, and time for collaborative team planning. Respecting teacher time requires a focused effort to first analyze the current schedule. What is working well and what are the shortcomings? After that analysis, the next step is understanding what teachers need, along with a collaborative effort to develop a schedule that meets these needs as closely as possible.

However, these efforts will be in vain unless teacher time is respected, used appropriately, and uninterrupted to the greatest degree possible. Respecting teacher time by not interrupting classes or planning periods unnecessarily is one particular area in which principal leadership is critical. Otherwise, schooling becomes a mere collection of independent teachers and support staff addressing their own needs and desires with little concern for the effect on the time of others. Two recurring culprits are frequent unnecessary announcements during classes and frequent meetings that fill the needs of administrators but take away from valuable teacher time.

The next chapter (page 85) discusses in more detail how collaborative teaming respects and protects teacher time. We frequently hear reluctance from some that collaboration takes too much time. In reality, when teachers are members of an effective team, they actually save time by collaborating. They collaboratively develop unit plans that are the basis for unit planning every year, and they develop and score common assessments. Each of these collaborative activities end up saving teachers time in the long run.

High-Quality Training

Teacher teams are frequently asked to perform unfamiliar tasks. Leaders who care make sure teacher teams receive the training they need to perform their work with a high degree of quality. Two particular areas in which teachers may require training are unpacking standards and developing common formative assessments.

Unpacking standards is an integral part of the work of teams in a PLC (DuFour et al., 2024). Teams work together learning how to interpret state standards and identify the essential outcomes for *all* students in every course, subject, and unit, reaching consensus on what each essential standard would look like in student work.

Teacher teams are also likely to require training in collaboratively developing common formative assessments. Teacher teams in a PLC need to learn how to develop formative assessments that link directly to the essential standards they have unpacked. Importantly, teacher teams must learn how to collaboratively analyze the results of formative assessments and link their analysis directly to providing each student additional time, support, or extension of their learning.

If students learn at different rates, doesn't the same hold true for adults? More specifically, do *teams* of adults learn at different rates? The answer is a resounding *yes*! It is unrealistic to think that every teacher team will perform with the same degree of effectiveness at the same time. Caring leaders understand this fact and will collaboratively develop plans for additional time and support for some teams, while other teams will need support to extend their effectiveness. There is a huge difference between recognizing that teams learn at different rates and in different ways and creating an effective plan to provide additional support for teams. Caring leaders move from knowledge to action.

In addition, if leaders value training and professional learning, they must participate in the professional learning themselves. In our consulting work, we have been in too many situations in which the principal or superintendent introduces us with great fanfare and then leaves the room. What message does this send to staff? By contrast, school leaders who sit in the front row during a training, taking copious notes, show that they are truly lifelong learners, even though they may be seen as masters of the subject being discussed.

Finally, as the heading to this section suggests, the quality of teacher training, both at the university level and in district-sponsored conferences, needs improvement (National Academy of Education, 2024). Unburdened by evidence and research, speakers often tell their life stories without taking a moment to consider the needs of the group. We encourage facilitators to begin each session with the request that participants devote just four minutes to completing this sentence:

"This seminar will be a success if . . ." A well-prepared facilitator will have anticipated what participants expect to get from the training and are prepared to deliver. In our experience, by far the most common way teachers complete that sentence is, "This seminar will be a success if I get at least one good idea that I can implement tomorrow."

Policies, Procedures, and Practices That Support Care

Policies, procedures, and practices are essential for embedding a caring culture in a school or school district. *Hoping* that those who make up a district or school community will behave in a caring manner is not the same as *embedding policies and procedures* that become "how we do things here."

We urge schools that haven't done so to collaboratively conduct a "procedures for caring" audit. The purpose of such an audit is to ensure that policies and procedures align with a message of "we care." Typically, such audits will reveal policies that promote cultural caring, policies or procedures that need minor adjustments, and some that may need to be eliminated.

Appropriate and Meaningful Compensation

Employee compensation is a critical part of any organization. It is counterintuitive to communicate to teachers how important they are and how much they are cared about, yet not provide appropriate and meaningful compensation. We often hear the phrase that "teachers need and deserve *adequate* compensation." The word *adequate* hardly communicates that teachers are valued.

While recognizing that dramatically increasing pay is not enough to reenergize the teaching profession, without increased pay, other efforts will ring hollow. Richard Ingersoll, Elizabeth Merrill, Daniel Stuckey, and Gregory Collins (2018) provide compelling evidence that the primary reason teachers leave the profession is their working conditions, not just compensation.

As the COVID-19 crisis demonstrated, even very substantial increases in compensation—some teachers called it "combat pay"—were insufficient to stanch the national teacher shortage. This shortage continues, years after the end of school closures, to negatively impact teachers who have remained on the job, as they lose collaborative time and professional learning in order to cover the classes of absent teachers.

While most district and school leaders may be unable to influence change in teacher compensation, they can focus on other teacher needs, such as working to boost teacher respect, improving feedback, strengthening leadership, building efficacy, allowing autonomy, and fostering collaboration (Reeves, 2018).

Structural aspects of schools and districts such as the examples discussed above are essential to creating a culture of caring, but by themselves they are inadequate. Viewing schooling though additional lenses is essential. For example, the *human* side of organizations must be examined.

Psychological and Human Needs

Imagine a school or district organizational chart that reflects the organization's structure. Such a chart would contain things like titles, job descriptions, and arrows to indicate who reports to whom, regardless of who fills each position. Now, realize that every position on the chart is filled by an employee—an individual human who brings to their position such personal attributes as their own unique background, experiences, personality, needs, and desires. In other words, a structural view, while necessary, does not account for the *human* side of an organization. Viewing teacher needs through a human relations lens is essential for creating a caring culture.

The human relations frame has a huge impact on teacher motivation. Understanding this fact explains why increasing pay for teachers, while necessary, is not enough. Teachers need (and deserve) respect from the larger public. The need for respect is an innately human need (Baumann, 2007; De Cremer & Mulder, 2007).

When working in schools, we are often asked, "Why can't the United States perform as well as Singapore, China, and other nations in international comparison?" Our uniform response is that those places don't have smarter kids or only brilliant teachers. They don't have more money and don't spent more time in class—in fact, many high-performing nations devote less time to seat work. What, then, is the "secret sauce" of these successful education systems?

The answer is *respect*. Whether it is Finland or a rural province in China, teachers are seen similarly to the way that clergy are treated in parts of the United States or the way military officers are treated around the world. This respect is reflected in the way that parents support teachers, in contrast to the prevailing attitude in the United States that, if the student has a problem, it is the teacher's fault.

Leaders at the national, state, district, and school levels proclaim a recognition of the importance of meeting teachers' psychological needs, but few will implement specific plans to do so. We declare how important teachers are to our society, yet we fail to act in ways that reflect such a belief. We must address the most basic psychological needs of teachers, and an excellent place to gain shared knowledge of these needs is through Abraham Maslow's (1954) work on motivation and personality, which identifies people's need for belonging, self-esteem, and self-actualization.

Belonging

Once an individual's physiological and safety needs are met, Maslow (1954) postulates that a higher order psychological need—the need for love and belonging—will emerge. This is an emotional need for interpersonal relationships, affiliation, connectedness, and being part of a group. Examples of these needs include trust and acceptance.

In schools, addressing teachers' need for belonging begins with recognizing the importance of collaborative teaming. Schooling has become so demanding and complex that even the best teachers cannot successfully work in isolation by themselves. Teachers need the help, support, encouragement, and shared learning that can only occur if schools are organized into high-performing teams, which is one of three big ideas of the PLC process. (In the next chapter, we delve deeper into the critical role collaborative teaming plays in a caring culture.)

Teacher teaming is not the only way teachers gain a sense of belonging, however. Cultural caring requires that meeting teachers' needs for belonging extends beyond being a team member. Appropriate leadership from the principal and teacher leaders impacts teachers' feelings of belonging. Leaders must embed structures and activities that allow teachers to communicate on a personal level with each other, get to know each other, and have fun together.

The core of such a culture is creating meaningful ways that teachers interact with each other, not just about professional issues, but personal ones as well. Cultural caring implies that teachers feel free to speak up and share their ideas, concerns, successes, and need for help. There must be mechanisms in place to communicate and address (or recognize and celebrate) individual teachers, needs for help.

The United States Marine Corps provides an example. There is no such thing as a "retired Marine." Marines remain a Marine for the rest of their lives. Marines, regardless of their age, care for their fellow Marines. There are numerous examples of Marines coming to the assistance of Marines who are experiencing difficulty in their lives. The Marine Corps motto of *semper fidelis*—always faithful—sums up what it means to be a United States Marine. Every Marine has a responsibility to care for their fellow Marines, both professionally and personally. Few things could be worse for a Marine than letting a fellow Marine down. Such a focus on belonging should be the goal of every school and school district, and that can only happen with strong and determined leadership.

Self-Esteem

If teachers' need to belong—to be part of a greater whole—is fulfilled, a higher order psychological need will emerge: the need for self-esteem. Self-esteem is associated with emotional self-confidence, self-worth, being capable, being useful, being necessary, and being valued by others. In short, teachers have the need to be recognized and appreciated for doing a complex and difficult job well, under increasingly difficult and challenging conditions.

It is important to note that the term *self-esteem* is sometimes misunderstood. We have heard teachers refuse to give a student constructive feedback on a task because "I didn't want to hurt her self-esteem." That attitude only leads to a false self-esteem in which anything less than praise can be devastating. Real self-esteem, by contrast, is built when teachers and school leaders provide accurate and specific feedback, accompanied with the words, "I believe in you, and I know that you can do better. Let's try it right now!" Similarly, we have seen administrators complain about ineffective teachers. When we ask, "What did that last teacher's evaluation look like?" in the vast majority of cases—in some states more than 99 percent—the evaluations are rated as "effective." While there is a common complaint about unions protecting bad teachers, we find that behind every tenured ineffective teacher there were administrators who failed to deal with performance problems directly and effectively. We have never seen a teacher evaluated into better performance, but we have seen many teachers coached into better performance. Genuine self-esteem comes not from an annual performance review, but rather from incremental feedback that gives teachers specific direction and next steps about how to improve their professional practice (Marshall, 2024).

Self-Actualization

Self-actualization is often misunderstood. At the most basic level, it refers to a feeling of fulfillment, of being content and satisfied with what you are doing with your life. Teachers need to believe in themselves, know that what they are doing is important, and perceive that they are making a significant contribution to the lives of others. Teachers alone cannot create conditions in their schools to self-actualize. Cultural caring requires leadership and respect from others.

The essence of self-actualization is clear evidence of impact. This does not always happen in real time, however. For example, veteran teachers experience evidence of impact when they hear from former students who communicate the teachers' positive influence on their learning. New teachers, however, might doubt the degree to which they make a difference. Leaders can provide evidence of impact by writing letters of thanks to teachers who made a difference for them, and they can ask current students to do the same.

We should note that Maslow's approach to organizing human needs is only one way to think of teachers' psychological needs. Such an approach, however, is a helpful way to organize discussions about what teachers need and how those needs can best be met.

Political Needs

On first thought, it might be difficult to wrap your head around the notion that teachers have political needs. However, if we carefully examine any organizational chart, including schools, we will see that each position is filled by an individual who has their own unique values and self-interests; thus, all organizations are inherently political. There is often tension between individuals' desires and values and an organization's broader interests and goals. This tension raises issues of power, decision making, resource allocation, and conflict resolution. In other words, political issues.

To be clear, the intention is not to remove politics from schools and school districts, but rather to recognize that organizational politics exist, and managing the political frame in a professional, effective way that benefits both the organization and individual is no small task.

The most powerful tool leaders have for addressing teachers' political needs is collaboratively developed, shared organizational commitments. In other words, when leaders engage the faculty in a process that addresses the question, "What commitments must we make, collectively, to become the kind of school or district we proclaim to value?" they are able to then use the shared commitments to resolve political issues when they arise. The shared commitments become the guardrails within which everyone has agreed to work and the attitudes they have agreed to exhibit (DuFour et al., 2021).

How does this look in the day-to-day life of a school? Here is an example: Perhaps one of the shared commitments a school has developed is "Each teacher will be a contributing member of a collaborative team," and an individual teacher does not want to be part of a team. They might prefer to work in isolation and have the attitude of "*my* students and *your* students" when it comes to collaborating on teaching and learning. It is not unusual to encounter resistance to collaborating and teaming. Some teachers might feel they will lose their autonomy as part of a team. They might feel shy and exposed in an uncomfortable way. They might feel they are more effective than their colleagues and have nothing new to learn. Whatever the reasons, this puts the principal in an awkward position: The school has collaboratively developed a shared commitment to teaming to fulfill their larger mission and vision, yet the principal also wants to meet the needs of individual teachers.

In such a situation, the principal might meet with the teacher in private and listen carefully to the teacher's feelings about the issue, asking for clarification as needed. Once the teacher has communicated their concern and the principal has a clear understanding of the teacher's position, the principal should review the school's commitment regarding teacher teams and explain why collaborative teaming is important.

The principal can then move the conversation forward by asking the teacher if there is anything about this commitment that they do not understand or that is not clear. This can be followed by the principal asking, "Is there anything I can do to help you meet this commitment?" and "Is there anything you need?" However, the critical point is this: The principal *must not equivocate on the expectation* that the teacher honor the commitment that is expected of everyone. Failure to take this step and let an individual teacher opt out communicates to everyone else that individual needs (or the power of an individual's personality) is more important than the needs of the school. In such a case the leader is sacrificing the will of the larger group for the will of the individual. Such conversations are difficult and require a leader to have excellent interpersonal skills. Using collaboratively developed, shared commitments moves political decision making and disputes from power struggles between the principal and the teacher to a more positive interaction.

Shared commitments are not only a powerful tool to use when addressing issues between individuals and the larger organization, but they are also a useful tool to implement in conflict resolution between individuals. Again, the question is, "What collaboratively agreed-on shared commitments did we make to create the kind of school culture ("how we do things around here") that will help us fulfill our organization's mission and values?"

Symbolic Needs

Another way to examine teachers' needs is using the symbolic frame. This frame considers the symbolic practices in schools that motivate educators and help us see that others care about what we do and how we do it. Symbolic practices include recognition and celebrations, stories that are told, and rituals that become part of the fabric of a community. One of the most important ways we learn what an organization truly values is through these symbolic practices.

Peter Drucker (1992) writes that reward, recognition, and celebrations communicate a larger message. He further notes, "Changing habits and behavior requires changing recognition and rewards . . . [because] people in organizations tend to act in response to being recognized and rewarded" (p.195). In short, while teachers need to be recognized and celebrated, what and whom we recognize and whose behavior we celebrate should be planned, purposeful, and meaningful rather than a random, spur-of-the-moment activity.

In schools, symbolic practices should align with the school's and district's mission, vision, values, and goals; that is, what the district is dedicated to accomplishing. This might seem like something every school would do—these things are worth celebrating. However, in our experience, schools often focus more on celebrating the wrong things. Two examples come to mind. First, a secondary school declares high levels of student learning as the school's core mission. Yet when we examine the school's symbolic practices for recognition and celebration, it isn't student learning that takes center stage, but athletics. Another example is from institutions of higher education that frequently declare how important teaching is in their respective institutions. Yet when faculty are recognized with tenure and promotion, what really matters most is research, writing, and publications. Such disconnect sends a powerful message to teachers: "Do not believe what we publicly say we value—that is simply for public relations. Instead, see what we value by what behaviors we publicly and frequently recognize and celebrate."

Planning for recognizing and celebrating teachers is important. DuFour and colleagues (2024) propose that an effective plan contains these four elements.

1. An explicitly stated purpose of celebration
2. Celebrations that are everyone's responsibility
3. A clear link between the recognition and the behavior or commitment the school is encouraging or reinforcing
4. Opportunities to have many winners

DuFour and colleagues (2016) remind us that "The criterion should be the sincerity with which the recognition is given. A commendation should represent genuine and heartfelt appreciation and admiration. If sincerity is lacking, celebration can be counterproductive" (p. 224).

The idea of continuous improvement in a caring culture implies a journey that never ends. How can leaders continue to motivate teachers on a journey that never ends? The answer is by purposefully and collaboratively embedding concepts and practices that meet teachers' symbolic needs in every school and district.

When schools do not meet teachers' needs, it can add to the already significant issue of teachers leaving the profession and young people deciding not to enter it, culminating in a broken teacher pipeline, which can have devastating effects on students.

Restoring the Teacher Pipeline

The teacher pipeline is broken. Will (2023) states that in 2022 in the United States, there were 55,000 unfilled teaching positions and another 270,000 positions filled with underqualified people. The implications of the teacher shortage are severe, both for our children and our larger society. Teacher shortages have the following impacts on students (Elevate Education, 2022).

- Disrupts learning with an unstable environment
- Limits relationship development making it harder for students to connect with their teachers
- Hinders achievement when schools have to cancel courses or staff classes with staff who lack resources, preparation, or certification in the subject
- Lowers graduation rates

- Reduces educational opportunities with discontinuity in delivery of instruction
- Disenfranchises already marginalized students disproportionately, such as students of color, students with disabilities, students from low-income families, and students from rural communities

There is a growing consensus regarding the reasons for such a severe shortage, including issues such as low salaries, poor working conditions, threats to personal safety, a culture of toxic accountability for both students and teachers, student behavior issues, lack of respect and appreciation, and a general lack of support for public education, to name a few. Simply put, the entire teaching profession is in disarray.

So what can be done to restore the teacher pipeline and strengthen the teaching profession as a whole? Reeves (2018) offers seven keys to addressing the problem.

1. **Boost respect for teachers and the teaching profession.** There was a time when teachers enjoyed respect, not only from their students, but also from society at large. This attitude has largely evaporated. Politicians who could historically be counted on to be the ardent supporters of teachers, the teaching profession, and especially the need for a strong public school system have, in many cases, abandoned this view, and often opted for a move away from public schools to a position of taxpayer-funded support for private schools. This lack of respect for public school teachers and public schools in general must change.
2. **Improve feedback.** Many teachers view the prevailing methods of teacher evaluation and accountability to be deeply flawed. In many states, teacher evaluation has become so toxic that teachers just give up and decide to leave the profession. Although we know the principles of effective feedback (FAST: fair, accurate, specific, and timely) apply to adults as much as to students, many state-mandated evaluation systems violate each of these principles. Leaders must, therefore, provide feedback to

teachers that does not rely exclusively on flawed evaluation systems but rather provides feedback on a daily basis so that teachers know what they are doing that is effective and how they can improve.

3. **Strengthen leadership.** Leadership matters—a lot! It is highly unlikely teachers will have a high regard for their profession if they work in a system that allows weak and ineffective leaders to lead schools. Yes, there is a severe shortage of teachers, but there is an even greater shortage of highly qualified, effective leaders.
4. **Build efficacy.** Teacher *efficacy*—one's belief that they can make a difference—must be at the top of the list of actions for school leaders. When conditions in any profession become so dire that people conclude that things are so bad they can't possibly make a difference, then leaders must address those conditions that cause people to lose their sense of self-efficacy.
5. **Allow autonomy.** Increasingly in education, teachers are losing their ability to make decisions. Teaching has become a more prescriptive profession in which teachers are directed to perform their work in specific ways. Teachers become discouraged when they feel they cannot teach in creative ways. Teachers have been placed in the untenable position of doing what they are told, how they are told to do it, and then, when the results are disappointing, they receive the blame. Leaders should be explicit about three levels of decision making. First, decisions teachers have the discretion to make, such as how to check for understanding, group and regroup students, and reteach based on student needs. Second, tight requirements that teachers have flexibility in implementing but must implement, such as using collaboration in lesson planning and common formative assessment. Third, situations in which leaders must make the final decision. In some schools we have observed, the principal posts a

chart listing these decision levels, and teachers are often astonished at how much discretion they have. At the same time, leaders have clarity about the domains in which they have decision-making authority.

6. **Foster collaboration.** Simply put, given the complexity of today's schools, teachers cannot successfully work in isolation by themselves. High-performing collaborative teaming has become widely used in organizations of all kinds. Meaningful collaborative teaming is no longer a new idea or a fad, yet in too many schools, collaboration is not the norm. Teachers are assigned their students, given the state standards, observed against a predetermined list of teaching behaviors, and evaluated on the basis of their students' test scores on a nationally normed standardized test. Teacher isolation is a recipe for failure, for both teachers and their students.
7. **Raise the pay.** Teachers must have dramatically improved pay. The bottom line is that teachers are leaving the profession in droves because of low salaries. And, while teacher pay by itself will not fix the shortage problem, not addressing the issue of low pay will guarantee that teachers will continue to leave the profession and that there will be no new teachers to take their places.

Questions for Discussion

Hope and inspiration come from action; they do not simply "bubble up" from within. Impactful action—action that makes a systemic difference—requires leadership. Use the "Caring and Teacher Needs Questions for Discussion" in the reproducible on page 83 to reflect on your school or district.

Caring and Teacher Needs Questions for Discussion

1. How does your school provide for the physical safety of teachers and staff? What additional steps could your school take to meet this basic human need?
2. What rituals and celebrations are embedded into the culture of your school? Do these rituals continue despite leadership changes, or do they change with every school leader? How can you identify enduring values that will transcend every leadership change?
3. How do you define self-esteem? In what ways does your school provide self-esteem for students and teachers?
4. As you review Maslow's hierarchy of needs, do you think anything is missing? How would you modify his theory to meet the needs of students and teachers today?
5. What are the most important ways that educational systems demonstrate respect for teachers? What are some ways that the system could do even better?

CHAPTER 6

Caring Collaboration

The fundamental law of human beings is interdependence. A person is a person through other persons.

—Archbishop Desmond Tutu

Caring cultures and collaborative cultures are inextricably linked. While virtually every school has individual administrators, teachers, and support staff members who care, it is impossible to embed a culture of caring without a culture of collaboration. Although there is widespread agreement regarding the benefits of a collaborative culture (DuFour et al., 2024), many traditional schools exist that remain structured around individual teachers working in isolation. Collaboration is one of those concepts that many people say they believe in, yet they often fail to actually act in collaborative ways.

At least part of the reason for this gap between belief and doing is the lack of agreement about what collaboration, when done well and with fidelity, actually looks like. For example, some educators equate collaboration with frequently keeping everyone informed. Collaboration is not the same as frequent emails, newsletters, and meetings sent to keep everyone updated on what is going on and why. Similarly, effective collaboration is much more than having occasional meetings in which everyone has the opportunity to share opinions. Perhaps most importantly, collaboration is not synonymous with unanimity, where everyone has veto power.

What, then, is collaboration? DuFour and colleagues (2024) remind us that when we ask teachers to collaborate, we are asking them to engage in the following:

> A systematic process in which [teachers] will work together, *interdependently*, to analyze and impact their professional practice in order to improve their *individual and collective results*. A *systematic* process is a combination of related parts, organized in a *methodical, deliberate*, and *orderly* way, toward a particular aim. It is not intended to be invitational or indiscriminate. Those who develop systematic practices do not *hope* things happen in a certain way; they create *specific structures to ensure* certain steps are taken. (p. 68, emphasis added)

The most common structure schools implement to embed a collaborative culture in their organization is teaming teachers who teach the same or similar content. The reason we use the phrase *same or similar content* is that teachers must have an obvious reason to work together collaboratively. There is the expectation that team members will work "*interdependently to achieve a common goal for which they are mutually accountable*" (DuFour et al., 2021, p. 136, emphasis original to source).

How Collaborative Teams Promote Cultural Caring

Collaborative teaming, when undertaken with fidelity, sends the recurring message that *we care so much that we will work collectively* to ensure and support the learning of each individual student. Importantly, we will also support each other, both in our professional lives and our personal lives.

Working in collaborative teams also sends the message that we care so much we will learn best practices that will *potentially* work for us. We validate effective practices by gaining shared knowledge through action research. In other words, we will always work *interdependently* to gain shared knowledge. Pfeffer and Sutton (2000) remind us that "Interdependence is what organizations are all about. Productivity, performance, and innovation result from joint action, not just individual efforts and behavior" (p. 197). Kenneth W. Eastwood and Karen Seashore Louis (1992) note that collaboration is "the single most important factor for successful school restructuring" (p. 215). Practitioners support collaborative teaming to enhance student success.

The culture of isolation prevalent in traditional schools sends the message, "These are my students; other teachers in the school are responsible for teaching their students." In such a structure, there is only so much an individual teacher can do and know about each student. Conversely, if a teacher is a member of a high-performing collaborative team, each teacher can share what they know about all students, not just those who are assigned to them.

For example, if a student is struggling with an issue at home or feeling left out by their peers, a teacher might share the problem with the entire team. Or if a student is experiencing an issue with another student or group of students, the entire team can share what they know about the issue. This illustrates the first step a collaborative team takes together when it comes to caring and supporting *all* students: gaining shared knowledge.

After learning from each other everything they can about students' issues or problems, the team can work together to agree on what actions to take to support the student. Such a collaborative process of student care and support is not a one-step process. After offering suggestions and agreeing on a strategy, the teacher and the team must monitor progress and continually adjust as needed.

Perhaps nowhere does collaborative teaming support students more than aligning student learning and behavior with additional time, support, and extension of student learning. Collaborative teams review the results of their collaboratively developed, common formative assessments and decide the most appropriate support or extension for each individual student.

In most traditional schools, analyzing student learning and providing appropriate support or extension are left to the individual teacher. Since every teacher has their unique strengths and weaknesses, the quality of analysis and support depends on the individual teacher to whom a student is assigned. The "luck of the draw" is a major factor in determining student success in traditional schools.

Collaboration through teaming not only enhances the care and support for students, but for teachers as well. When teachers are members of a high-performing collaborative team, they are part of a professional team in which the whole is more than the sum of the parts. Most importantly, teachers help and support each other professionally. They learn together. They collaboratively plan together. They learn the benefits of developing, analyzing, and using the results of common formative assessments. They share teaching strategies, ideas, and materials, and they take *collective* responsibility for results.

Teaming shouldn't stop with learning and support within the team, however. It should extend to other teams throughout the school, or even throughout the larger district or at state or national levels at meetings. Teams in a PLC—a *professional learning community*—not only learn together, they also share their work with others. Visit the AllThingsPLC website (AllThingsPLC.info) to team with leaders and educators from across the United States and the world.

How Collaborative Teams Support New Teachers

Nowhere is the effect of collaborative teaming's care and support more visible than in the impact on new teachers. Given the accelerated pace of teacher turnover, care and support for new teachers are more important than ever before. Consider how new teachers are typically inducted into the profession. After an interview, they are hired, they meet with the principal and perhaps their department or grade-level leader, they are given the pertinent documents, such as the state standards and class rolls, and perhaps assigned a mentor. The approach often seems to be much like the proverbial, "let them sink or swim." This approach is the antithesis of caring and supportive.

In a PLC, new teachers are hired as members of a collaborative team—the third-grade team, the fifth-grade team, the mathematics team, and so on. New teachers are interviewed by the team and the team members share their views about each candidate's likelihood to be a successful *team member*. Once a new teacher is hired, the team shares their collaboratively developed lesson plans and formative assessments, and the school's plan for care and support for each student who is experiencing difficulty, along with the school's plan for extending the learning of students who have demonstrated proficiency. As the team approaches each new unit of instruction, team members share teaching strategies, materials, and—importantly—insights into some students' specific needs. In short, new teachers enter into the profession as part of a caring culture and a member of an efficient and effective team.

While a culture of collaboration is a powerful tool for enhancing care and support for teachers professionally, collaborative teaming, when done well, can have a positive effect on the emotional well-being of team members. As team members work together to improve student learning and behavior, the very act of working together and taking collective responsibility for their professional results provides a structured opportunity for team members to get to know each other on a personal level, incrementally building trust and caring.

Working together, solving problems, and celebrating the positive results of their efforts incrementally leads to a culture of personal trust. We are often asked, "How do we build trust?" The answer may seem like a cliché, but it holds true: *The way to create trust is to act in a trustworthy way.*

Once members of the collaborative team begin to establish trust with each other, they will begin to open up and share more about their personalities. As a result, over time, teachers will share with the team their personal successes and struggles. In a high-performing team, teachers feel emotionally safe, cared for by their fellow teachers, and supported on a personal as well as professional level.

How to Reconcile Vigorous Debate With Mutual Respect

How does a collaborative culture reconcile the inherent tension between respect for teacher autonomy and vigorous debate yet maintain a culture of mutual respect? Researchers and practitioners such as Thomas J. Peters and Robert H. Waterman Jr. (2006) and DuFour and colleagues (2024), among others, advocate for a culture that is both loose and tight, signifying autonomy within parameters. By collaboratively developing agreed-on commitments—*norms*—schools and teams can encourage both vigorous debate, autonomy, creativity, and individual ownership of the loose aspects of teaching and learning within the parameters they have previously agreed on while remaining tight on the big ideas of a PLC—a focus on learning, collaborative culture and collective responsibility, and results orientation (DuFour et al., 2024).

Schools have a long history of developing belief statements. Virtually all accrediting agencies in our profession require schools to develop a mission statement, and almost all mission statements represent a set of beliefs. Do schools need to clarify and articulate their core beliefs regarding their mission—their central purpose? Absolutely! But absent agreement about what we are *willing to do* to fulfill our mission, the effectiveness of belief statements is severely limited.

Collaboratively developed *shared commitments* or *norms* lay out in writing what individuals within the school and each team are willing to do. These are typically written as *We will . . .* statements. Usually few in number, these statements typically articulate the boundaries within which everyone agrees to work. For example, shared commitments for a school might be similar to these examples from the faculty at Adlai Stevenson High School in Lincolnshire, Illinois:

- We will develop curriculum and instructional strategies that utilize various resources, which will promote active involvement of students and provide for their varied experiences as well as their individual abilities and talents.

- We will assist each student in his or her transition into high school, through high school, and beyond by providing appropriate instruction, monitoring his or her progress, and offering guidance and support services tailored to individual needs.
- We will model the importance of lifelong learning through our ongoing professional development.
- We will collaborate with one another to create conditions that provide equity and promote student success. (DuFour et al., 2021, p. 353)

Here are some other examples of shared commitments at the team level.

- We will focus on the learning and behavior of each student.
- We will monitor each student's progress skill by skill and provide each student with effective and appropriate additional time, support, or extension of their learning.
- We will accept responsibility for the learning of all students, not just those to who are assigned to us individually.
- We will provide input for team agendas, and we will distribute agendas for meetings prior to each team meeting.
- We will start meetings on time and end at the designated time.
- We will actively listen and respect the views of all team members.
- We will support each other professionally and personally.
- We will continually monitor team effectiveness and seek to continually improve our effectiveness.

Of course, shared commitments can only be effective at building mutual respect if teams use them. This means collective commitments must be monitored. Periodically, agendas should include items such as the following.

- How are we doing as a team?
- How can we improve our relationships with each other?
- Are there examples of caring and support for each other or our students that went above and beyond what we would normally expect? How can we recognize, celebrate, and reinforce these behaviors in frequent and meaningful ways?

A word of caution is in order: Although utilizing the power of collective commitments can be an effective way to balance the inherent tension between vigorous debate and mutual respect, they will lose their effectiveness if leaders are not willing to confront behavior that is incongruent with the commitments faculty members have made to each other. Ironically, developing a caring culture through autonomy within defined parameters requires more leadership, not less—just leadership of different kind (DuFour & Fullan, 2013).

How Collaboration Works in a PLC at Work

The PLC at Work process (DuFour & Eaker, 1998; DuFour et al., 2024) has been one of the most successful and resilient approaches for enhancing student achievement. While multiple reasons account for the success of the PLC at Work process, one characteristic that stands out is the use of collaborative teaming to embed a collaborative culture throughout the school. Collaboration is the engine of the PLC at Work process.

Collaborative Teaming

It is virtually impossible to develop a meaningful collaborative culture without effective structures that embed collaboration as a way of life in a school. In *Corporate Cultures*, Terrance Deal and Allan Kennedy (1982) define *organizational culture* as "how we do things around here." In the PLC at Work process, "how we do things," both structurally and culturally, is through the power of collaborative teams.

Among the earliest to recognize the need for modern organizations to work collaboratively as a "learning organization" were Peter Senge, Richard Ross, Bryan Smith, Charlotte Roberts, and Art Kleiner (1994). Senge and his colleagues observe, "Teams are recognized as a critical component of every enterprise—the predominant unit for decision-making and getting things done . . . Working in teams is the norm in a learning organization" (pp. 354–355). To be more accurate, Senge and his colleagues might have added, "Except in America's system of public education."

Many researchers and writers have joined the call for collaborative teaming. For example, Kathleen Fulton and Ted Britton (2011) emphasize the importance of collaborative teaming as follows:

> We now have compelling evidence that when teachers team up with their colleagues, they are able to create a culture of success in schools, leading to teaching improvements and student learning gains. The clear policy and practice implication is that teaching is a team sport. (p. 4)

Organizing Teams

While there is no one correct way to organize teachers into teams, there are three aspects of effective teaming to consider. First, do team members have something in common that will have a positive impact on student learning? This typically means teams should, when possible, be composed of teachers who teach the same or similar content. We have heard teachers experience frustration when they are placed on a team with no apparent commonality.

Second, the organizational structure of teaming in a school must be monitored for effectiveness, and necessary adjustments must be made. The initial team structure in schools, while collaboratively developed, is still a best-guess scenario. Once team members begin working together, it might become clear that adjustments are needed here and there. A full academic year should not go by without teams making needed improvements. We should not let an entire group of students suffer the consequences of inaction.

Finally, everyone must be a contributing member of a collaborative team. We must recognize on the front end that not everyone will be enthusiastic about being a member of a collaborative team. Some teachers will express the desire to "just give me my students and leave me alone." This is just one area in which the power of schoolwide shared commitments, coupled with an effective leader, matter—a lot!

School size and grade level will determine the most effective organization of teacher teams in individual schools. To the degree possible, teams should be organized around teachers who teach the same course or grade level, such as social studies teams or fifth-grade teams. In smaller elementary schools, teams are often organized vertically—perhaps a K to 3 team, and a 4 to 6 grade-level team. Some teams function as interdisciplinary teams, although, unless members are using interdisciplinary units, the teachers will have little in common except the students. However, there can be great value in interdisciplinary teams if the purpose is clearly articulated, as when teaching writing across the curriculum, for example. For singleton teachers who are the only ones teaching a particular subject, electronic teams can be valuable resources. The COVID-19 pandemic taught us that effectively connecting with others on a regular basis and having meaningful collaboration are possible remotely using virtual tools.

Again, the question should not be "Have we organized into teacher teams?," but rather, "Have we organized into teams in such a way that they can effectively enhance student learning as well as adult learning as a team?"

Team Training and Coaching

It is unreasonable to expect successful collaboration as a team without effective training and ongoing coaching. In the PLC at Work process, being a member of a collaborative team involves much more than merely meeting together and sharing ideas. Teams in any organization should engage in work that will enhance their likelihood of success. In a PLC, this means doing the right work—work that will have a positive impact on student learning and behavior, along with work that will continually enhance individual and team growth.

Adults, like students, learn at different rates. Not all teams will progress at the same pace. After receiving initial training, some teams will need additional coaching on various aspects of collaborative teaming. Since the very concept of *continuous* improvement implies a never-ending process, effective coaching must be ongoing. The goal is to enhance the effectiveness of *each* team. Thomas W. Many, Michael J. Maffoni, Susan K. Sparks, and Tesha Ferriby Thomas (2018) put it well when they write the following:

> If collaborative teams are to be the fundamental building blocks of a PLC (and they are), and if collaborative teams in PLC schools are going to focus on the right work (and they must), then the leadership team of the school must work to ensure collaborative teams have everything they'll need to be successful in the work they must do. (p. xvi)

The first step that members of teams in PLCs always take is learning together. Developing high-performing collaborative teams requires collaborative learning and focused coaching.

Collaborating on the Right Work

At first glance, it might seem obvious that teams must collaborate on the right things. In the PLC at Work process, there is clarity about the work of teams, and collaboratively developed, shared commitments form the boundaries of how teams will do the right work.

While collaborative teams are often pulled in many directions, they maintain a sharp focus on the core purpose of the school: the learning of each student, skill by skill. To ensure that they maintain this focus, most of a team's work revolves around four critical questions directly connected to student learning:

1. What do we want our students to learn and be able to do in each course and unit? What is essential that all students learn? What would student learning look like in work that demonstrates proficiency?
2. How will we know whether each student has learned and can do what is required? How can we monitor along

the way, through common formative assessments, each student's progress?

3. How will be respond, as a school and as a team, when students struggle in their learning? What systems are in place to connect individual students with focused additional time and support?
4. How will we celebrate, extend, and enrich the learning of students who demonstrate proficiency in their learning? How do we prevent "under learning?" (Eaker & Keating, 2015).

Teams will collaborate on other important matters too. They will plan common units for student learning by collaboratively analyzing data from formative and summative assessments. They will set improvement goals and monitor their progress toward goal attainment throughout the year. They will monitor and improve their effectiveness of providing additional time, support, and extension of learning for their students. Importantly, they will discuss students' personal challenges and work collaboratively to help in various ways, such as by involving school counselors, school psychologists, and other support personnel both within and outside of the school.

We cannot overemphasize that team members often collaborate on how to help and support each other both professionally and personally. For example, they support each other professionally by sharing ideas and materials, while on a personal level, they collaborate by listening deeply, encouraging, and offering to help teammates. Teachers also need someone to recognize and celebrate their accomplishments, even those that might seem small. Like school leaders, teams need to create, among themselves, lots of winners and celebrate their success frequently in meaningful ways. Many things account for the sustained success of the PLC at Work processes, but embedding collaboration through high-performing teams is indispensable.

Finally, collaboration requires trust. Every teacher and leader we know believes that they are trustworthy, and we believe them. Nevertheless, schools are hierarchical organizations and hierarchy breeds distrust. Therefore, we ask you to consider one additional behavior, drawn from James M. Kouzes and Barry Z. Posner's (2011) book *Credibility*. In their landmark research with more than one million leaders across the globe, Kouzes and Posner (2011) reduce the essential element of credibility to the belief that leaders will do what they say they will do and expect every team member to do the same. Here are some examples:

- "At our last meeting, I promised to bring you data and research on student writing. Here they are."
- "At our last meeting, we all agreed to bring examples of authentic student work so that we can work on collaborative scoring. You did it! Thanks for being so conscientious."
- "At our last meeting we agreed to bring a case study of a student who is struggling and ask our colleagues for support. Thanks for being courageous enough to do this."

Leaders doing what they say they will do creates a rhythm of promises made and promises kept. It is one of the best ways we know to create and maintain leadership credibility.

Questions for Discussion

This chapter focused on the impact teamwork and collaboration have on creating a caring culture in PLCs. Use the "Caring Collaborations Questions for Discussion" in the reproducible on page 98 to reflect on your school or district.

Caring Collaboration Questions for Discussion

1. Describe your most successful experiences with team collaboration.
2. What are the barriers to effective team collaboration?
3. What is one thing you have learned in the past year that was new to you? How did you share that insight with your colleagues?
4. What is something that you believed was true about teaching and learning five or ten years ago but now know is no longer true?
5. What are the characteristics of the best professional learning you have experienced? How can that experience be replicated in the future?

CHAPTER 7

Caring Leadership

When the leader's work is done, the leader's aim fulfilled, people will say, "We did it ourselves."

—Lao Tzu

We both served in the military: Bob was in the United States Marine Corps, and Doug was a battery commander and intelligence officer in the United States Army. We had the chance to serve with some great leaders, as well as some not-so-great ones. Among those we would rather forget were the leaders who relished the power and prestige that came along with every *sir* and *ma'am* more than they felt drawn by the responsibility to serve their country. But we also served with leaders who were kind, compassionate, and caring. They were the first to comfort a fellow Marine or soldier who had suffered a loss while far from home. They noticed when those they led were not themselves, when their mood or motivation was low or their frustration high, and they responded not by barking commands but by taking a genuine interest in helping fellow soldiers. Most importantly, these great leaders were relentlessly focused on supporting the next generation of leaders, never jealous of others or fearful that acting with selflessness would jeopardize their opportunities for promotion.

Doug's brother, Major General Steve Reeves, was one of the great ones. He led a decade-long effort to provide defense from chemical and biological weapons around the world. Despite very long days working to fulfill this duty, Major General Reeves always fulfilled his other responsibility to care for his fellow service members. There was a tradition that a general officer would meet every flag-draped coffin arriving at Andrews Air Force Base outside of Washington, DC. These arrivals often happened at two or three o'clock in the morning. Being a leader who cares, Major General Reeves saw this tradition as every bit as important as his job keeping the world's population safe from chemical and biological weapons.

Great leaders such as Major General Reeves have empathy. It is probably easy to see, as the examples from our military service show, how empathy is a critical part of leadership in a caring culture. Empathy will do little, however, if leaders do not also have high expectations for those they lead and clarity about the decision-making structures they have put in place in their district, school, or department.

The Empathy Question

Empathy is often confused with sympathy. *Empathy* (n.d.) is "The action of understanding, being aware of, being sensitive to, and vicariously experiencing the feelings, thoughts, and experience of another." People who have empathy can understand without having gone through the feelings, thoughts, or experiences themselves. Consider some religious traditions that have empathy at their core: to weep with those who weep and mourn with those who mourn. Believe it or not, there have been those who argue against leading with empathy. For example, the startlingly titled book *Against Empathy* by Paul Bloom (2016), a Yale professor of psychology and cognitive science, notes that many problems individuals and organizations face are not due to a lack of empathy, but rather because of too much of it. We believe that much of the disputes over empathy are based on imprecision in our language, in which empathy and sympathy are sometimes used interchangeably. *Sympathy* (n.d.) is "a feeling of sincere concern for someone who is experiencing something difficult or painful." With empathy, we are actively sharing another person's emotional experience. To get a better understanding of sympathy, consider what you see on your computer screen if you do an Internet search for the phrase *expressing sympathy*. You'll see links to funeral home web pages and florists, along with suggestions for how to express your condolences.

Here's the essential difference for leaders in education: When leaders empathetically address an issue such as teacher or student underperformance, they put themselves in the shoes of the other person, offering constructive advice or feedback to assist, promote resilience, and help the teacher or student get back on their feet, supporting them in their ability to do better in the future. Stanford psychologist David Yaeger (2024) provides excellent examples of empathetic feedback. This feedback is accompanied by the explanation, "I'm providing this statement because I have confidence in you and know that you want to use this feedback to improve" (Yaeger, 2024). Whether the context is middle school students, surgical residents, or NBA players, this sort of empathetic feedback had a measurable impact on the performance of those receiving the feedback. A leader in a culture of caring would not simply soothe the sting of disappointment with a bouquet of flowers or a condolence card. Stanford professor of psychology and neuroscience Jamil Zaki (2019) notes that empathy is not a fixed trait. However, he warns against superficial empathy assessments, often in digital form, that provide the illusion of support without the essential three-dimensional relationships on which empathy must be based. Computerized feedback in the form of artificial intelligence (AI) has limits; it provides insight into right or wrong answers but fails to give students specific strategies on how to improve their performance. While AI can assist teachers in many ways, it will never replace real relationships. Genuine empathy, Zaki (2019) argues, is a skill one develops, not something one learns by reading a book or attending a workshop.

One of the of the most important empathy-building practices that leaders can use is avoiding practices that undermine empathy. The best example of this is teacher evaluation. While laws and policies often require a particular form of evaluation, it is often a major source of friction between teachers and leaders. While leaders surely must follow the law, we have never seen a teacher "evaluated into" better performance. But we have seen many teachers receive coaching, with consistent feedback and support, who dramatically improve their performance by reducing failure rates, improving classroom climate and culture, and improving their own job satisfaction. Empathic feedback is frequent, supportive, and consistent.

Finally, we argue that kindness and goodness are essential elements of real empathy. While traditional definitions from dictionaries and psychology texts emphasize the cognitive elements of empathy—understanding the perspective of another—we wish to establish a caring framework for the term. Our bottom line is that even if you think an action is empathetic, if it's not kind, it may feel affirming and warm, but it is not empathy. For example, it is not kind for a leader to give false affirmation to a teacher, like setting up a junior faculty member for the denial of tenure after six years of labor in the lab, or assuring students that they are doing wonderful work right up until the moment that student fails the class. Almost every reader of this book has been a first-year teacher. We can recall the feeling we had at the end of the school day as first-year teachers when we wondered, "Can I succeed in this profession?" The empathic leader's response to that question is not, "Of course! You are wonderful! You are great!" Rather, an empathic response would be, "I am confident that you can be a great teacher, and I can help you improve your skills to achieve that goal."

In addition to being empathic and doing what they can to develop their empathy skills, leaders in a caring culture also have high expectations for adults and students.

High Expectations

It is often said that people's performance will rise or fall based on the expectations held for them, whether they are good or bad. The best evidence of the power of high expectations goes back to a Harvard study in the 1960s conducted by psychologists Robert Rosenthal and

Lenore Jacobson (1966). In the experiment, teachers received randomly assigned IQ scores for students. A year later, those students rose or fell to the level of their randomly assigned scores (Aucejo, French, Araya, & Zafar, 2020). While there has been academic controversy surrounding the original study, there is little doubt that the preponderance of evidence demonstrates that expectations are strongly related to performance and, by contrast, that low expectations can lead not only to low performance but also catastrophic consequences. Whether the environment is a classroom or an airline cockpit, when the leader assumes a command and control position, students fail to ask questions and flight crews fail to challenge the captain, even when facing the risk of deadly decisions from the captain (Edmondson, 2018).

The most important consideration with high expectations is that leaders (and others, including teachers and parents) express those expectations in a certain way. Consider hearing, after an especially difficult failure, "You can do anything you set your mind to!" or "You always miss that one!" The first presents an unrealistic expectation and the other is belittling. It is imperative that we define with clarity what expectations mean, veering away from both unrealistic and too-easy goals. In their book *The Progress Principle*, Teresa M. Amabile and Steven J. Kramer (2011) offer compelling research on the sweet spot of expectations. They find that rather than identifying unrealistic expectations like "win the championship" or "write a *New York Times* bestseller," people are better served by meeting small, incremental goals that they can make progress on day by day, consistently taking steps forward (Amabile & Kramer, 2011).

These ideas are illustrated in music classrooms where, with every breath, the conductor provides incremental feedback: "louder, softer; faster, slower; higher, lower." In a fifteen-minute observation, leaders can hear improvement in the quality of students making music. Similarly, great coaches do not wait days or weeks to provide feedback but provide in-the-moment support to each student to improve their stance at the plate, make a better tackle, or take a granny shot to improve their free-throw percentage.

In addition to setting appropriate expectations, leaders in a caring culture must also communicate clarity in their decision-making structures.

Clarity in Decision-Making Processes

School leaders make a dizzying number of decisions every day, from how to conduct a classroom observation to how to set the agenda for a faculty meeting to how to differentiate professional learning based on the needs of each teacher. They must make decisions that consider various perspectives and demands, developing a decision-making process that is transparent and fair. For example, consider how some leaders conduct staff meetings. We have often seen leaders who wax eloquent about the value of interaction between teachers and students and rail against teacher lectures and then lecture staff in faculty meetings with little interaction. A better practice is one that we observed from a principal who, committed to faculty interaction, ended each agenda item with a question mark rather than a period. This principal was clear that the purpose of meetings was deliberation and inquiry, not passively listening to announcements. Before the meeting even started, this leader set the tone that active engagement is an essential part of staff meetings and adult learning, just as it is in the classroom.

A transparent process ensures that everyone knows which decisions will be made by whom—which decisions are the prerogative of the leader, which are collaborative, and which are made by teachers. Reeves (2021a) conducted a study in which he found that teachers perceive that more than 90 percent of decisions are top-down mandates and that they have little discretion in their daily classroom decisions. Nevertheless, actual observation of classroom decision making revealed that 39 percent of decisions—such as how to group, regroup, stop a lesson, reteach, and so on—were discretionary. Only 27 percent of decisions were administratively directed, and the remaining 34 percent were collaborative (Reeves, 2021a). If teachers believe they have no say in decision making, they might feel as though the culture is not a caring one and that they are not valued or respected.

In schools with caring cultures, leaders make decisions that involve values and safety. Leaders do not need to convene a focus group or get consensus to address, for example, fire safety, cafeteria hygiene, and bus safety. Similarly, if a school maintains equity and high expectations as core values, then its leaders have the responsibility to make decisions in cases where equity is in question, such as with socioeconomic status or ethnicity. When, for example, there are a disproportionate number of low-income students who are failing classes and the leader discovers the primary cause of failure is missing homework, then the leader has an obligation to move the school toward practice being done in class rather than at home.

Collaborative decisions include decisions team members make together in meetings, as when they develop and score common formative assessments, an essential ingredient in schools that have implemented the PLC at Work process (DuFour et al., 2024). Participants must also have clarity from leaders about each person's role in the group as they consider important decisions (Mankins & Garton, 2017). For example, some participants are there to share their expertise, especially in areas such as technology, finance, and law. Other participants might offer their insights about compliance with laws and local board policies. But the most challenging element of developing a decision-making structure is who the ultimate decider will be. It may be a process of group consensus or majority rule. But in some cases, the leader is the decider. The other participants in the meeting offer their expertise and insight, but the leader alone bears the responsibility for making the final decision. A little bit of time at the beginning of a meeting to make sure participants understand the decision-making process prevents unnecessary dissent and disappointment.

In *The Surprising Science of Meetings*, Steven Rogelberg (2019) finds a number of common flaws in meetings that prevent leaders from effective decision making. For example, many meetings include too many participants who are there not to offer deliberation and inquiry, but only to have face time with the leader. Jennifer Sparrow, deputy superintendent of Singapore American School, has meetings down to a science, with each agenda item associated with specific participants. When their part of the agenda is completed, these participants leave. This replaces what could have been a four-hour-long meeting with twenty minutes of direct engagement in an agenda item on which they had expertise (Reeves, 2020b).

Another technique we have noticed in meetings with effective leadership decision making is to have every agenda item end with a question mark rather than a period, as we noted earlier in the chapter.

Leaders can expect participants to read documents in the meeting folder on a shared drive or watch brief video presentations associated with each agenda item before the meeting so that there are no death-by-PowerPoint presentations during the meeting. This way, the purpose of the meeting is for deliberation and inquiry, followed by a considered decision.

In the PLC at Work process, there are three levels of decision making. The first is teachers' discretion. For example, teachers may make decisions about questions such as, How do I group students? When do I stop a lesson and reteach? How do I provide immediate and specific feedback to students? The second level is collaborative. For example, collaborative teacher teams agree on common formative assessments and strategies for academic support. The third decision level is where the administrator makes the call, typically on issues of values and safety. As one teacher told us, "We don't need to vote on fire drills." Similarly, if a school has a core value of collaboration and sharing, then leaders do not tolerate practices that undermine those values.

Motivation Through A+ Players

For their book *Time, Talent, Energy: Overcome Organizational Drag and Unleash Your Teams Productive Power*, Michael Mankins and Eric Garton (2017) studied thousands of organizations to determine how leaders manage people's time, talent, and energy. They came to a conclusion about employee motivation: The best employees (what they call A+ players) benefit from the opportunity to work with other A+ players. Leaders in caring cultures must clearly distinguish between performance that is acceptable (you won't get fired) and performance that is exemplary. An example of this differentiation in teacher performance levels is Kim Marshall's (2019) teacher evaluation rubric (see chapter 5, page 63). Leaders find ways for educators who have a high level of skill in a certain area or leadership potential to collaborate and learn from others who also have high skill levels. These great teachers can not only have a significant impact on school performance but also can magnify their personal and professional satisfaction if they are allowed to take leadership roles. These leadership roles do not require a title, but rather the opportunity to lead colleagues in the best way, with influence, modeling, and local evidence of impact. Consider the benefits of supporting A+ players by having them work on real-time challenges collaboratively for professional development with other teachers rather than, for example, receiving the same mandatory training sessions required for first-year or substitute teachers. The former is a vastly more effective professional learning model (DuFour et al., 2024). This will inevitably mean that some high-performing teams are more effective and efficient than others. These teams can act as models for the entire organization.

Questions for Discussion

This chapter identified key leadership qualities that best foster caring cultures. Use the "Caring Leadership Questions for Discussion" in the reproducible on page 108 to reflect on your school or district.

Caring Leadership Questions for Discussion

1. What are the characteristics of the best leaders with whom you have worked?
2. Every school has some A+ players—the teachers and leaders who not only have great results but also encourage and support colleagues. They are often not recognized. How can you recognize, encourage, and increase the A+ players in your school?
3. How does your school demonstrate high expectations for students and adults? What are the warning signs that there are low expectations for students and adults?
4. In your last team or faculty meeting, how were decision responsibilities clarified? What was your role as a contributor?

CHAPTER 8

Caring Governing Boards

The principles of effective governance include integrity, transparency, and collaboration.

—From the United Nations' "Principles of Effective Governance for Sustainable Development"

Much of what happens in schools is the result of decisions made by various boards that govern educational systems. Nations have turned to their education systems to address some of their greatest challenges. In the United States, these include educating the masses to support a functioning democracy, desegregating society, and meeting the technological challenge posed by the Soviet space program, to name but a few. Each of these challenges required action on the part of educational governing boards that cared enough to direct the country's moral compass toward facing these challenges.

Certainly, there is no shortage of governing boards setting the direction of America's public schools, including everything from congressional educational committees, the U.S. Department of Education, state legislative education committees, state boards of education, and local boards that direct each school district. It is interesting to note that while many question the effectives of today's schools generally, national polls show satisfaction with local schools (Conway, 2024). There is little or no criticism of those who have the legal (and moral) responsibility for ensuring a high-quality education for *every* child who attends America's schools. To the extent that they can be held accountable, governing boards are susceptible to board member elections, which are often influenced by political agendas rather than educational performance.

The challenges in America's education system are significant; the following are only a few possible examples.

- Ensuring schools are safe for both students and adults
- Guaranteeing both excellence and equity for every student
- Replenishing a dwindling teacher supply with competent and caring individuals
- Meeting the challenges stemming from rapid advances in technology
- Restoring faith in our schools and professional educators
- Turning the tide of government support for funding a dual system of education in the United States—one public, one private—with public tax dollars

Arguably, America's school system is in crisis, Now, perhaps more than ever, we need America's governing boards to care enough to meet the daunting challenge of saving the country's system of public education.

Successfully addressing the challenges requires governing boards that are dedicated, with members who are willing to look beyond their individual experiences and views to pursue a larger vision for the greater good. Such a vision can motivate, restore, and reignite a belief in our educational system. In short, we desperately need governing boards, at both the state and local levels, that care passionately and deeply.

Caring at the Top

While recognizing teachers need caring leaders, it is not unusual to immediately focus on either the position of principal, superintendent, or both. While no one would argue about the critical importance of these positions in creating a caring culture, we should recognize that cultural caring begins with local school boards. In many ways, the school board and superintendent *team* is the most important team in a school district, since the quality of their work—their caring—will impact the effectiveness of all other teams throughout a district. Karin Chenoweth (2017) echoes this point when she observes "District leadership shapes the conditions in which schools operate and as such can support or undermine school success and thus student success" (p. 14).

The behaviors of the school board and superintendent team matter—a lot! If collaborative teams are to be the engine that drives behavior and attitudes throughout a school district—every school, every team, every classroom—then the school board and superintendent team is no exception and should serve as a model for school-based collaborative teams. Cultural caring starts at the top.

It is interesting to note that in a PLC, everyone is expected to engage in meaningful, timely, and specific training. However, in many districts, training is expected of everyone except the school board and superintendent team. Beyond modeling for others, there are practical examples of why the school board and superintendent team need training—some of them are legal, and many are simply practical ways the team can be more effective. In short, the school board and superintendent must commit to doing more than simply meeting and discussing.

Cultural caring from the top down begins with gaining shared knowledge by listening deeply and learning together. A caring school board does more than merely listen and then average opinions. The board members also do the following.

- They become deeply engaged in learning about the high-priority goals of schools and teams.

- They monitor the progress schools and teams are making on a frequent and timely basis.
- They also focus on things that are not working well.

In other words, cultural caring involves listening and learning together—caring enough to pay attention. This is the only way the school board and superintendent team can then set meaningful and attainable district goals.

Ensuring Safety

While many things contribute to the flight from public schools, parents fearing for their children's safety is a major factor (Rock, 2024). The enrollment decline is pervasive, with 14 percent of students leaving public schools going to private schools and 26 percent to home schooling (Rock, 2024). Teachers who choose to leave—or not enter—the profession also note safety as a reason (Ingersoll et al., 2018). More than half of teachers surveyed believe that their sense of safety has decreased while less than 10 percent said that their safety has increased (Peetz, 2023). Writing for the National Education Association, Brenda Alvarez (2023) reports the following:

> One-third of the teachers reported being threatened by a student within the year, including verbal threats, cyberbullying, intimidation, or sexual harassment and 29 percent reported at least one incident from a parent. Fourteen percent of teachers said they have been victims of physical violence from a student.

Unlike many aspects of schooling, such as curricula or methodology, concern for physical safety is not an abstract concept. In 2023, there were 346 school shooting incidents in the United States; that is almost one per day (Korhonen, 2024). As tragic as shooting incidents are when they happen in schools, students are much more likely to experience gun violence at home or in their local community—especially if they live in an area of high poverty (Panchal, 2024). Research suggests that schools are often safer than other environments where young people spend their time. A study published in *The Journal of Pediatrics* found that adolescents are at a significantly higher risk of experiencing violence in their homes, neighborhoods, and communities compared to schools (Haasz, Boggs, Beidas, & Betz, 2022).

While there is no shortage of opinions regarding why these violent acts happen, governing boards, at every level, have the responsibility to move beyond analysis and make every school safe for every student and adult. It is only when schools *become safe* that the public will return to the belief that schools *are safe*. Governing boards must show that they are interested in creating a safe environment for students and staff and then convince teachers and the public at large that schools are safe places to learn and work.

There are practical things governing boards can do to support a greater sense of safety in schools for teachers, students, and parents.

- Clearly establish discipline policies to reduce ambiguous and frustrating consequences for student misbehavior.
- Ensure a visible administrator and faculty presence in the hallways during passing periods and at the beginning and end of the school day.
- Analyze data on the locations and times of day for disruptive behavior.

Standing Up for Employees

Given the number of schools and students in the United States, it is not surprising that educators—particularly teachers—are easy targets for criticism. Criticism of U.S. schools and teachers is not new. What *is* new is the lack of strong support for educators and our system of free, public education from politicians at every level, as the annual survey by Phi Delta Kappa consistently reports (PDK International, 2024).

Historically, during times when schools (and the teaching profession) have undergone attack, the one group whose support educators could count on was our elected politicians and members of our various governing boards. This is no longer the case. In fact, there is an increasing number of politicians who have chosen to attack public schools as a popular campaign tactic—particularly when coupled with calls for using tax money to support enrollment at private schools. Too often, local school boards are alarmingly quiet.

Leaders at every level must realize the magnitude of what is at stake: nothing less than America's system of public education for all. Our schools—in fact, the United States as a whole—need leaders who will stand up and not only defend educators, but also publicly honor them at every opportunity. They deserve our public appreciation and respect. The most important decision that governing boards can make is to protect staff members from abuse. This requires a school board chairperson who, for example, will expel people from the public comment portion of a board meeting when attendees devolve into making abusive comments about school staff.

Curriculum in schools remains the exclusive province of states and local districts. Because education is not mentioned in the United States Constitution, the Tenth Amendment makes clear that powers not enumerated in the Constitution are reserved to the states (U.S. Constitution, amend. X, § 1.). That is why fifty states have fifty different assessments and fifty different sets of academic content standards. This places a particular burden on state and district leaders and their governing boards to provide a curriculum that not only is rigorous and appropriate but also meets the political demands of voters. Bob and Doug were both deeply involved in the educational standards movement of the 1990s that sought to establish clear, measurable learning goals consistently across the United States and hold schools accountable for student performance. Despite the efforts of federal legislation, such as the No Child Left Behind Act, states have remained staunchly possessive of their exclusive responsibility for curriculum and assessment policies. Governing boards and senior administrators, therefore, bear the burden of communicating with the public about how their curriculum and assessment policies meet the needs of their students.

Addressing Policies and Practices

Conditions and circumstances change over time, but policies and procedures often stay in place. "That's the way we've always done it!" is a refrain heard often in education, from the boardroom to the classroom. Rarely does a new superintendent, building principal, faculty member, or support staff person get to start their work in an organization with no previous history of policies or procedures. The same is true of governing boards. Practically all districts and schools have a myriad of policies, procedures, and practices that have evolved over many years.

Charles E. Lindblom (1959) popularized the term "disjointed incrementalism" to describe how policies and practices accumulate, incrementally, over an extended period of time. Since governing boards, superintendents, principals, and teachers adopt policies and procedures ad hoc, incrementally, year after year, the result is often a number of policies and procedures that have become outdated or disjointed and can have unintended negative consequences. Even the most well-intentioned policies and procedures can have unintended consequences. Perhaps educators didn't take a detail into account when they adopted the policy or procedure, or new knowledge might have become available since adoption. Whatever the reason, policies and procedures that have a negative impact, even when unintended, must be identified and addressed.

Educational systems vary widely in their approach to these challenges. While some governing boards leave assessment matters to the administrators and educational experts that they employ, many others are subject to virulent attacks during public comment periods over politically charged curriculum topics. Practical things that school leaders and governing board members can do include the following.

- Be very clear about what is, and what is not, in the curriculum.
- Publicly share examples of test items and student responses. We have found it especially helpful when board members and the public can see how student performance improves over time instead of static performance data that show a moment in time.
- Welcome public comment and parent review of curriculum documents, textbooks, and assessments. We have observed that part of the resentment from parents and other voters about education is that they perceive a

veil of secrecy on these matters. Board members and other leaders must attempt to lift this veil.

Policies for Local School Board Meetings and Public Discourse

Local school board meetings are one of the key places for public discourse about our schools. However, just as in district, school, and team meetings, discourse should occur within parameters and not dissolve into a free-for-all. School boards benefit greatly when they have developed a policy for public comment at board meetings. Figure 8.1 provides an example of such a policy.

Policy for Public Comment in Board Meetings

Civil society requires that we engage with those people and organizations with whom we disagree. We follow the principle of seeking first to understand before seeking to be understood. That can only happen in an atmosphere of vigorous but respectful debate. The other side of the argument might be misinformed and deeply wrong, but that does not make them evil. They deserve both a vote and a listening ear as much as any other constituent. What they do not deserve is the right to bully and threaten those with whom they disagree, and that is why senior leaders and policymakers must establish and enforce the rules of civil discourse. Here are some examples of such rules that governing boards and senior leaders might consider.

1. The purpose of public comments during governing board meetings is to allow citizens of the district to share their ideas and for the board and district leadership to learn from those citizens. We welcome different opinions, vigorously argued, provided that expressing those opinions falls within the boundaries of civil discourse as outlined in this policy.
2. Speakers at governing board meetings must be residents of the district and provide proof of residency when they submit their names for recognition during the public comment period.
3. Speakers must address an educational issue directly relevant to this school system. General political speeches not related to education are not relevant to the decisions of the governing board.
4. Speakers may not make any threats, explicit or implied, to any staff or board member, either inside or outside the meeting, either directly or indirectly, or either in person or via any electronic means, such as social media.

By signing into the application to speak at public meetings, the applicant agrees to abide by these policies and agrees to ejection from the meeting if the applicant fails to abide by these policies.

FIGURE 8.1: Sample model policy for public comment in local school board meetings.

Process for Cultural Caring That Protects Teachers, Administrators, and Support Staff

Teachers and support staff need direction, and they especially need direction in a caring culture. This is best accomplished in a cyclical process that is both top down and bottom up. Eaker and colleagues (2021) describe this cyclical process:

> The cycle begins with the school board and superintendent team. Based on an in-depth analysis, as well as feedback from all teams at other levels, this team develops both short-term and long-term high-priority goals for the district. These goals, along with policies, set direction and align the work of teams throughout the district. Year in and year out, this top-down–bottom-up process becomes essentially one of data and input flowing up, and policies, goals, directions, and resources flowing down.

When the school board or superintendent team develops clear ways of doing things and models a culture of caring, those who work within the school district community feel a sense of security, confidence, and protection. They feel that the school board and superintendent team are more than a collection of individuals who each have their own separate agendas.

The shared commitments that the school board and superintendent team make to each other, the administrators and teachers, the support staff, and the larger community, are a more direct way for the school board and support staff to protect everyone within the school community. In effect, these collaboratively developed, shared commitments communicate the message, "To become the kind of educational community we seek to become, these are the commitments we will promote, protect, and defend—day in and day out." Importantly, when administrators, teachers, and support staff see the school board defend these commitments, they become believers. Time and again, the message is sent: "You can depend on us to protect you as you work in a caring culture guided by the shared commitments that we made to each other."

Policy and Procedures Audit

In complex organizations such as school districts and schools, there is no real alternative to disjointed incrementalism, since the term describes how, over time, policies and procedures are developed. What governing boards, superintendents, and principals can do is periodically focus on the current effects of policies and procedures, regardless of how or when they were developed.

We suggest districts and schools conduct a policy and procedure audit, which is a deep analysis of the policies and procedures currently in place. Such an audit should be a collaborative effort, conducted by those who work in the district or school, with each policy or procedure ultimately listed under one of three categories.

This policy or procedure . . .

1. Is needed, with no changes
2. Is needed, with changes
3. Is not needed and should be discontinued

Any district or school will have a great number of policies or procedures, and it will take time to audit each one. We suggest beginning with the policies or procedures that are the most visible, have the greatest impact, and are frequently utilized. Examples include the following.

- Personnel policies and procedures that involve teacher recruitment, hiring, and evaluation
- Policies, procedures, and practices related to testing, grading, and reporting pupil progress
- Organizational structure and responsibilities
- Professional development policies and practices
- Curricula policies
- Instructional planning and implementation

Again, these are only a few examples of the kinds of policies and procedures that often have unintended negative effects, and it is the governing board's responsibility to address such issues. Truly effective leaders are willing to take action—even actions to *stop* doing certain things (Reeves & Eaker, 2019).

It is one thing to identify policies and procedures that need attention; it is another thing to address them in a way that is likely to yield positive results. Gaining *shared* knowledge—learning together—should be the first step in addressing policies and procedures that need revision. For example, the issue of grading reform is challenging and complex. We advocate that school boards and superintendent teams research and learn about best practices for grading from multiple sources *before* making major changes in grading policies and procedures.

Importantly, shared learning should not stop with adopting new changes. We encourage educators to engage in action research on particular policies and procedures once implemented. They should keep in mind questions such as, What are we learning as we implement new approaches? What adjustments do we need to make? What did we not think about? In other words, *every new policy or procedure carries the potential for new unintended consequences.* Ongoing action research is one way to deal with this problem professionally, promptly, and importantly, by local practitioners.

Questions for Discussion

This chapter examined how governing boards can support school leaders as they implement caring practices. Governing boards at every level of education have an obligation and an opportunity to enhance the success of every teacher, and the profession as a whole, and thus the learning of each student. For stronger public advocacy for our schools, we need boards that govern within a caring culture where caring is visible at the top, safety is ensured, governing bodies stand up for employees, and policies and practices are created and maintained to ensure positive effects. Use the "Caring Governing Boards Questions for Discussion" in the reproducible on page 120 to reflect on your school or district.

Caring Governing Boards Questions for Discussion

1. What, if any, personal interactions have you had with school board members? To what extent were those interactions related to the daily realities of classrooms and schools?
2. How does your school board protect faculty and staff from abuse during public comment periods and on social media? What policies have they created to guarantee respect and protection for staff members?
3. How have you been engaged in school board elections? What restrictions, if any, have been imposed on you as a school employee in public advocacy for matters that come before the school board?
4. How does your school board hear about success stories from your school?
5. How are students' voices represented in your school board meetings?

CHAPTER 9

Leading With Care—Five Essential Decisions

There is a big difference between understanding the value of the people inside an organization and actually making decisions that consider their needs.

—Bob Chapman and Raj Sisodia

The very concept of leadership implies decision making. It follows, then, that the quality of leader decision making has an impact—good or bad—on the culture of any organization. Although leaders make countless decisions every day, some decisions have a greater impact on organizational culture than others. We think the following five decisions are crucial for effective leadership.

1. How will we determine our priorities?
2. How will we decide what to stop doing?

3. How will we recruit, reward, and retain our best teachers and leaders?
4. How will we engage parents, community members, and policymakers in a vision for educational success?
5. How will we embed values to provide continuity and consistency beyond leadership change?

We will discuss these five decisions in the following sections.

How Will We Determine Our Priorities?

Determining educational priorities does not require a strategic plan or complex needs analysis. Leaders need to consider two contrasting visions: (1) the pain of change and (2) the pain of failing to change (Reeves, 2021a). For example, the pain of change isn't uncommon when there are changes in curriculum, when there are changes to assessment practices when teachers already feel over-tested, or when there are political pressures restricting the choices for students who require academic support. Change can be very painful and overwhelming, but we too seldom consider the alternative—the pain of failing to change.

- More than 1.1 million students left school during the school closures associated with the COVID-19 pandemic and have yet to return to school (Mervosh & Ngo, 2024).
- COVID-19 caused grave learning loss for students with long-term consequences (Mervosh & Ngo, 2024).
- At a time when schools need support for students who have fallen behind, they find themselves with slashed budgets and now must cut staff, close schools, and increase class sizes (Mervosh & Ngo, 2024).

Some schools and educational systems will make the tough calls, eliminating initiatives and programs that have little value, cutting extraneous curricula, and focusing on helping students succeed and survive; most importantly, they will persuade students who have left the system to return to school. But we fear others will continue to spend until the money runs dry. We predict that there will be bankruptcies at the local, district, and state levels, as has happened in the past with disastrous results. Pensions were cut and government services were reduced. If governing boards do not act with courage to establish priorities now, it may be too late in future months and years. And, as with most undertakings in a PLC at Work culture, setting priorities should be a collaborative, data-driven, research-based process.

First, leaders must determine their priorities. However inspiring positive visions may be, we conclude that leaders must also create a negative vision of what the future will be if the system fails to change. There is substantial psychological evidence that negative images are more persuasive than positive ones (Tierney & Baumeister, 2019). In the short term, it is easy to resist essential changes, particularly when those changes are inconvenient and require changes in schedules and feedback systems. But in the long term, our duty is not to the naysayers of today, but to the students of tomorrow and of future generations.

How Will We Decide What to Stop Doing?

Most school and district planning documents are full of goals, tasks, and commitments. In *The 100-Day Leader*, Reeves and Eaker (2019) insist that before leaders and teachers undertake any new goals, tasks, and commitments, they must create a "not-to-do" list. We frequently meet with resistance on this requirement: "Everything I do is important, and I can't give up anything!" We remind our colleagues that the end of the school year will arrive, barring Armageddon, and there will always be tasks that are left undone. Therefore, the only choice is the conscious not-to-do list, the path we recommend, or the unconscious not-to-do list—whatever leaders and teachers did not finish because they just ran out of time. The reason so many schools lack the resolve to create common formative assessments and engage in collaborative scoring protocols is not a lack of will or skill, but rather that they failed to eliminate other low-priority tasks from their overwhelming to-do lists.

There are some easy-to-follow rules for the not-to-do list. First, start small. You need not eliminate hours of work in a single action.

Instead, focus on smaller actions, such as the needless responses to emails and texts within thirty seconds when responding in three to four hours will do very well. Many meetings are automatically scheduled for an hour on most scheduling software, but they could be completed in forty-five minutes. Multiply that saved fifteen minutes by the number of minutes that you have in a year and you save days and even weeks of time.

One challenging but easy addition to the not-to-do list is meetings that duplicate other meetings, are unnecessary, or do not require the presence of every participant. Deputy superintendent Sparrow had sat in too many four-hour meetings in which the contributions of individual members only required twenty minutes. Because of this, she creates a very tight agenda in her meetings; if your presence is only required for twenty minutes from 2:20 p.m. to 2:40 p.m., you are done—no need to attend the whole meeting. This respects participants' time and keeps the meeting focused.

We know of a Wisconsin principal who has an annual "dumpster day" in which she looks through files for things like twenty-year-old word searches from reading curriculum tools that are no longer useful, and they go into the dumpster. It is not possible to complain that "we don't have the time" when we continue to cling to time-consuming activities that are no longer necessary. We have seen leaders make their overwhelming to-do list visible on a whiteboard in their offices, and then invite colleagues, including administrative staff and faculty, to find something that they could volunteer to do. These stretch assignments help develop the next generation of leaders and also relieve leaders from the all-or-nothing fallacy of "either I must do it or it will never get done."

Here is the bottom line: If you are unable to complete a not-to-do list, you will never achieve this year's goals, no matter how lofty and compelling those goals may be.

How Will We Recruit, Reward, and Retain Our Best Teachers and Leaders?

Although the teacher shortage is undeniable and the pipeline of students in teacher preparation programs is shrinking, we have seen some very creative ways to address these challenges. In some colleges, student teaching, or clinical practice, begins in the first year of college, not the last year. If a student learns that they do not like to be around difficult students or deal with the challenges of high-poverty schools to which they are likely to be assigned, then a decision in the first year of college to change majors is much easier than the same decision made in the last year. We have seen interview processes that include asking prospective teachers to come to the interview prepared to teach a forty-five-minute lesson to a specific grade level to which that teacher might be assigned. These classes take place in the schools where the newest teachers are most likely to be assigned. The interview is then scheduled for the afternoon, and some of the prospective teachers decide after the teaching experience not to continue with the interview. This is a far more reliable way to assess future teacher competency than the typical interview in which they claim that their greatest weakness is that they care too much.

Recruiting great teachers is only the start of restoring the profession. The long-term challenge is retaining those teachers. In too many systems, the only way to get an increase in compensation is to go into administration—the worst reason we can imagine to become an administrator. The good news is that more districts are starting career ladders in which a master teacher, who is willing to coach and support colleagues, can earn as much or more than an administrator. Educational policymakers make a grievous mistake when they lure the best and brightest teachers out of the profession to go into administration, a job for which their teaching expertise may not be well suited. While we need administrators who are instructional leaders, that expectation does not always match reality. Schools certainly do need instructional leadership, but that role may or may not be played by administrators. To retain great teachers, administrators must ensure that they are compensated in a way that allows them to pay the mortgage and educate their children, which are goals not always within the grasp of a typical teaching salary.

Finally, we must not overlook a major source of teaching talent: retired educators who, while still in the early fifties, have thirty or more years in the typical retirement system and therefore have no incentive to remain on the job. Policymakers must reform retirement policies so that teachers can continue to earn a good salary, increase their retirement income, and most importantly, make great contributions to students and schools.

How Will We Engage Parents, Community Members, and Policymakers in a Vision for Educational Success?

In too many schools, parents and community members have been alienated from schools. Some examples include attacks on school libraries over books that protestors find objectionable, even when books the protestors objected to were not in the libraries. Many protests have been launched against perceived taught subject matter, even though no state standard includes the subject matter. One would hope that a simple statement of facts would be sufficient to quiet inaccurate protests, but school leaders and teachers must do more. There are many damaged relationships to repair, and that healing begins with parents and community members knowing that educational systems listen to and respect them. The message is not, "You are wrong, and we are right," but rather "We know that you love your kids and want the best for them, and so do we. Let's work together to provide the best education possible for your students."

How Will We Embed Values to Provide Continuity and Consistency Beyond Leadership Change?

While change leadership dominates the titles of books for educational leaders, a missing element of these treatises is helping staff members and community leaders know what will not change. Almost every school and district have enduring values that should not be discarded with a leadership change. Nevertheless, we have frequently seen situations in which teachers interpret the arrival of a new leader as a sign that past curriculum and instructional practices are now in question, even when those practices are demonstrably effective. This can lead to institutional paralysis. "We can't do anything until we know what the new superintendent wants," they claim. We ask, "What are the chances that the new superintendent will want a lower literacy rate? What are the chances that the new superintendent will want a higher dropout rate?" Therefore, it is the responsibility of today's leaders to be clear about what will not change and what policies and practices must be sustained even when leadership changes.

Questions for Discussion

In this chapter, we have presented five critical leadership decisions. Use the "Leading With Care Questions for Discussion" in the reproducible on page 128 to reflect on your school or district.

Leading With Care Questions for Discussion

1. List the top three priorities of your school and district (if you are studying this book in a collaborative team, ask your colleagues to do this independently). What are the greatest pain points for schools and communities? What priorities are the same and which priorities are different? What accounts for the differences in priorities?

2. Consider writing an initiative inventory, listing all the instructional, curriculum, assessment, and leadership initiatives in your school and district. How are the responses to this challenge different between classroom educators and school and district administrators? Try to identify just two or three initiatives that can be terminated to better focus on your greatest priorities.

3. What incentives have led your best and brightest teachers to remain in the profession? What factors have led great teachers to leave the profession?

4. When parents and community members have been very supportive of schools, teachers, and local leadership, what accounted for that support? When parents and community members are not supportive, what accounts for that lack of support?

5. What are the enduring values of your school and system? What values and professional practices will remain in place five or ten years after you retire?

CHAPTER 10

Caring Communities and a Caring Nation

The quality of care we give to our parents, to our brothers and sisters, to our families, to our friends and neighbors, and to the poor and the powerless endows a life, a community with respect, hope, and happiness.

—Eunice Kennedy Shriver

In a democracy, schools are inherently political institutions. They reflect the values of their communities, including parents, the voters who elected the governing board, and the traditions that are deeply ingrained in school life. While we expect school leaders to be instructional leaders who observe classrooms, support professional learning, and establish clear criteria for recruiting great teachers and implementing learning, we also expect these leaders to engage in local civic activities and service clubs and build relationships with local employers and nonprofit organizations. Yet time is a zero-sum game: Every hour a leader devotes to one of these priorities is an hour taken away from another.

Throughout this book, we have discussed how leaders can build caring communities, but we must also acknowledge the expense of leaders constantly attempting to balance a priority with ten other competing priorities popping up at every turn. Building a culture of caring requires not only the dedication of senior education leaders, but also of leaders at every level, including teacher leaders, union leaders, parent leaders, and student leaders.

As citizens in a nation that has suffered schisms in politics, education, and civil rights, Americans have healed through a common vision that was greater than the schisms that had ripped us apart. In this chapter, we also explore the lessons of the past and what they might teach us about creating a culture of caring.

In an earlier chapter, we claimed that Maslow (1954) had it right: Safety is essential for learning. When students and community members do not feel safe, both physically and psychologically, matters of education take a back seat to safety. However, we argue that safety and educational success are integrally related. When, for example, students fail to complete high school, that is not a challenge for the current year's graduating class, but a fifty-year or greater challenge for the entire community. These students face a lifetime of unemployment, poverty, increased use of the medical care system, and increased involvement in the criminal justice system (Reeves, 2021b). It is therefore the responsibility of teachers and school leaders to demonstrate that school success is not just about test scores and grades but is instead a communitywide issue of safety. While the costs of education and intervention for students who have fallen behind are significant, those costs pale in comparison to the costs of providing the social needs of students who drop out of school (Alliance for Excellent Education, 2011).

Community Engagement and Civil Discourse

While leaders and governing board members generally seek to engage the community in educational matters, we have noticed a distinct change in the tone of engagement. That change is from a respectful dialogue and airing of divergent views to virulent attacks on teachers, administrators, and board members. Worst of all, these attacks include not only matters of policy disagreements but also attacks on the families of leaders and board members. Hardworking school employees report that they are followed to their cars with the menacing announcement that "We know where you live." A superintendent friend reported that after pictures of his home and family were posted on social media by a group critical of the school and district, he awoke to find his yard littered with garbage. Most people in education have developed a thick skin when it comes to accepting critical comments, but it crosses the line when, rather than civil discourse, there are threats and intimidation that extend to family members.

We offer some suggestions to governing boards and their chairs to address this growing concern.

- Move public comment to the end of the meeting so it does not impede the board's ability to first cover essential business.
- Have clear guidelines on public comments, such as the requirement that comments must relate to the agenda items at the meeting.
- Require that participants indicate in their public comment that they are residents of the district. This avoids the possibility of people from outside the district using meetings to further their own agendas.
- Require that the board chair shut the meeting down when the rules of civil discourse are violated.
- Organize sharing of the positive. In one district, the teachers' union collaborated with district leadership to have representatives from each school take turns coming to board meetings, arriving early to sign up for public comment to share with the community and board all the remarkable things that were going on in their school.

Building Bridges in Diverse Communities

One of the most persistent challenges in connecting communities to schools is the widely diverse cultures and backgrounds of the community and the schools that serve them. In many communities where the majority of residents represent a broad spectrum of race and cultures, it remains common for most teachers and leaders to be White. We do not advise hiring people based on race, but rather suggest that in these circumstances, we have a particular obligation to reach out to the community. In one district that won the national Broad Prize for Urban Education, district leaders made a commitment to attend Sunday services at churches that had predominantly African American members. Reverend Martin Luther King Jr. called eleven o'clock on Sunday morning the most segregated hour in America (King, 1958). It changes the perspective of White leaders to sit for a while where they are the only White person in the room. To be clear, these leaders were not there to make a speech or otherwise be recognized, but only to show their desire to be a member of the entire community. Fortunately, there is evidence that suggests that schools can provide community engagement and build academic success (Chenoweth, 2017). Specific strategies for community engagement educational leaders might consider include the following.

- Change the location of parent-teacher conferences from school buildings to neutral territory, such as community centers or faith community buildings.
- Invite parent and community leaders to help with community events, as speakers or translators, or to help with organization, such as scheduling or promoting events and preparing food.
- Make students an integral part of community engagement events through musical and dramatic performances.

If we wish to have better community engagement, then we must reject the angry exchanges, threats, and intimidation that sometimes characterize rhetorical combat between community members and school leaders and replace it with a requirement for civil discourse.

Along the way, we can build bridges between teachers and school leaders and the diverse communities that they serve.

Learning From Lessons of the Past

It is easy to care about people we love and about friends who generally agree with us. It's much more difficult to care about those who have deeply wounded us. Abraham Lincoln (1865) knew the power of reconciliation, as he shared in his famous words of his second inaugural address:

> With malice toward none; with charity for all; with firmness in the right, as God gives us to see the right, let us strive on to finish the work we are in; to bind up the nation's wounds; to care for him who shall have borne the battle, and for his widow and his orphan, to do all which we may achieve and cherish a just and lasting peace among ourselves and with all nations.

These words make the controversies of today sound trivial. For all the vitriolic rhetoric before local and state school board meetings, before congressional committees, not a single speaker could imagine the heavy heart with which President Lincoln, after losing hundreds of thousands of his countrymen on both sides of the war, urged not retribution or rancor, but malice toward none and charity to all. If we aspire to build a nation in which a culture of caring is our goal, then let Lincoln's words displace the angry vitriol that claims the center stage of educational rhetoric today.

Until the 1830s, education in the United States meant wildly different things to different schools, teachers, and governing board members. When William Holmes McGuffey published his set of *Eclectic Readers* (commonly known as *McGuffey Readers*) for primary students in the 1830s, he could not have known that for almost a century his books were as close as the United States would come to a national curriculum. *McGuffey Readers* taught students how to read with explicit phonics instruction more than a century before the science of reading came into vogue. McGuffey's books also taught explicit moral lessons about loyalty, hard work, and self-improvement.

Perhaps the least noticed lesson of McGuffey's books was the power of high expectations. We took some passages from *McGuffey's Third Eclectic Reader* (McGuffey, 1879, originally published 1836) and analyzed their reading level using 21st century tools. Astonishingly, the reading level for the passage we chose was 9.1. We expect the ninth-grade students of today to achieve what was expected of third-grade students in the 1800s. We have found that even when there are sharp policy differences in education, people of different viewpoints can frequently agree on the value of high expectations for all students.

When President Obama was running for office, a leading criticism of the young one-term senator was that his primary professional experience was as a community organizer. We wish that the United States had more community organizers and that aspirants to political office were praised rather than ridiculed for these essential skills. It is important to distinguish engagement from advocacy. If the only people invited to a community meeting are those with whom we agree, then genuine engagement is impossible. When, for example, community support is required to pass a bond proposal on the ballot, then supporters of the bond must interact with voters who have no children or grandchildren in schools. In one community, only 28 percent of the electorate had students in school and a high number of voters were senior citizens who felt disengaged from public education. Why spend more than fifty million dollars on a new school when the community senior center was in a dilapidated house? On the third attempt to pass the bond issue, the new school included a new senior center. Not only did the bond issue pass, but seniors were also able to volunteer in the school and, as they were closer to students and faculty, provide broad support for education throughout the community.

Examining Our Fundamental Values

There are cultural norms that cannot be constrained by geography. In his magisterial *Democracy in America*, Alexis de Tocqueville (2006, originally published 1839) contrasted his observations on the new American nation with his observations of European states. Despite the differences he found, de Tocqueville (2006) importantly noted that these vastly different nations with widely variable histories had, in many respects, common values and consistent elements deeply embedded into their culture. Many elements of the systems of governance, legislation, economics, and regulating moral conduct were remarkably similar across national and cultural boundaries.

For example, just as European nations maintained both laws and cultural codes to maintain family ownership of property and protect and treat elders with respect, early American legislatures also took steps to prevent the elderly from being robbed of their land, possessions, and dignity. Though de Tocqueville did not mention them, many Asian cultures have a deep respect for their elders. In China, for example, many communities have converted unused school buildings to "old people's universities," in which retired people play ancient instruments, maintain the practice of calligraphy, and offer spontaneous gestures of hospitality such as free concerts and art displays for visitors.

Other cross-cultural values include respect. In some cultures with monarchies, respect was granted to the agents of the crown, while in others, the highest level of respect is vested in the people, with no one elevated above another by virtue of heredity. Despite this clear difference, the underlying theme of respect remains a cultural norm. In some cultures, respect suggests deference to men while in others it is deference to women that is the cultural norm. In almost all cultures, with the exception of those in which a child is crowned with the privileges of royalty, children owe respect toward parents and other elders.

In creating a culture of caring, the responsibility of the leader is not merely to be a passive inheritor of the present culture, but rather to engage in acts of leadership that shape the future.

Shaping Future Generations

Among the many qualities that make teaching such a profoundly meaningful profession is the impact educators have on future generations. We are confident that readers who have taught for some time have had the wonderful experience of a former student contacting you and saying things like these.

> *"What you did for me in fifth grade helped me be a better college student."*
>
> *"What you did for me in high school helped me succeed and start my own business."*
>
> *"The way that you inspired me in kindergarten made me want to be a teacher just like you."*

Our priorities, therefore, are not just today's class or the week's faculty meeting or next week's board meeting. We measure our commitments not in hours or days but in decades. When we ask educators and leaders why they entered this profession, the most common answer we receive is that they wanted to make a difference. Truly effective educators know that effectiveness is impacted not only by what they do, but by who they are and the values they represent—day in and day out.

Questions for Discussion

This chapter broadened the scope of a caring culture, first to the local community and then nationally. Use the "Caring Community and Caring Nation Questions for Discussion" in the reproducible on page 137 to reflect on your school or district.

Caring Community and Caring Nation Questions for Discussion

1. What have been your most successful interactions with parents and community members? How can you build stronger bridges with parents and community members who have been critical of education?
2. What lessons of history are most important to your commitment as an educator or leader? If you are lucky enough to have parents or grandparents who recall the lessons of the past, ask them what they believe are the most important lessons of history.
3. How have you healed broken relationships? Abraham Lincoln suggested that we start "with malice toward none." How can we apply his guidance today?
4. What fundamental values do we want to pass on to our students? What values of the past, such as a commitment to racial injustice, do we want to reject?
5. How can we engage authentically with those we disagree with and use the lessons of history to help us come together despite those disagreements?

Epilogue

Basketball great Michael Jordan, perhaps the best player to ever step onto a court, was renowned for making the shot that led to victory. But whenever he was asked about his remarkable success, he reminded the interviewer that there were many more times when he was entrusted with the ball to make the winning shot and failed. When asked how he could continue in light of these statistics, he famously said, "You miss 100 percent of the shots you don't take." There is a lesson for readers who fear that some of the suggestions in the preceding pages might be too risky. What if I try something and it doesn't work? What if I provide honest feedback and it leads to a meltdown by the student or a colleague? What if parents resist and even resent my suggestions, telling me that I'm a teacher and not a parent? What if I take a risk in trying to create a culture of caring and then am criticized for it in front of the school board and community?

These and many other sources of self-doubt plague teachers and leaders and, worse yet, cause them to doubt themselves, paralyzing them at the very moment when thoughtful, decisive, and yes, risky, actions must be taken. So let us offer these gentle reassurances.

You will make mistakes.

You will make decisions in good faith and be criticized for them.

You will conduct yourself with integrity and professionalism and not receive a word of thanks.

You will be thanked for your dedication and caring years after the criticism has faded into history.

You will receive completely unexpected notes of appreciation from former students and colleagues when you least expect it.

You will reflect on a noble profession and a life well lived because you created a culture of caring.

We, Doug and Bob, thank you for joining us on this journey. We have both experienced all the joys and challenges of teaching and leadership. We enter the twilight of our careers confident that, despite our mistakes, we have made a difference. We hope that this book has made a difference for you as well as the students and colleagues that you serve. We leave you with the following story from author Eric Butterworth (Canfield & Hansen, 2001):

> A college professor had his sociology class go into the Baltimore slums to get case histories of 200 young boys. They were asked to write an evaluation of each boy's future. In every case the students wrote, "He hasn't got a chance." Twenty-five years later, another sociology professor came across the earlier study. He had his students follow up on the project to see what had happened to these boys. With the exception of 20 boys who had moved away or died, the students learned that 176 of the remaining 180 had achieved more than ordinary success as lawyers, doctors, and businessmen.
>
> The professor was astounded and decided to pursue the matter further. Fortunately, all the men were in the area and he was able to ask each one, "How do you account for your success?" In each case the reply came with feeling, "There was a teacher."
>
> The teacher was still alive, so he sought her out and asked the old but still alert lady what magic formula she had used to pull these boys out of the slums and into successful achievement.
>
> The teacher's eyes sparkled and her lips broke into a gentle smile. "It's really very simple," she said. "I loved those boys." (Canfield & Hansen, 2001, p. 5)

References

Ablon, J. S. (2018). *Changeable: How collaborative problem solving changes lives at home, at school, and at work.* TarcherPerigee.

Alliance for Excellent Education. (2011, November). *The high cost of high school dropouts: What the nation pays for inadequate high schools.* Accessed at https://all4ed.org/wp-content/uploads/2013/06/HighCost.pdf on March 25, 2025.

Alvarez, B. (2023, October 9). *Teaching in turmoil: The growing threat of student outbursts.* NEA Today. Accessed at www.nea.org/nea-today/all-news-articles/teaching-turmoil-growing-threat-student-outbursts on April 1, 2025.

Amabile, T. M., & Kramer, S. J. (2011, May). The power of small wins. *Harvard Business Review.* Accessed at https://hbr.org/2011/05/the-power-of-small-wins on October 2, 2024.

Aucejo, E. M., French, J., Araya, M. P. U., & Zafar, B. (2020). The impact of COVID-19 on student experiences and expectations: Evidence from a survey. *Journal of Public Economics, 191*, Article 104271. https://doi.org/10.1016/j.jpubeco.2020.104271

Audisio, A., Taylor-Perryman, R., Tasker, T., & Steinberg, M. (2023). *Does teacher professional development improve student learning? Evidence from Leading Educators' Fellowship Model.* Accessed at https://edworkingpapers.com/sites/default/files/ai22-597_v3.pdf on April 1, 2025.

Baldwin, J. (n.d.). *The blind men and the elephant.* Accessed at https://americanliterature.com/author/james-baldwin/short-story/the-blind-men-and-the-elephant on March 20, 2025.

Baumann, P. (2007). *Persons, human beings, and respect.* Accessed at www.swarthmore.edu/sites/default/files/assets/documents/philosophy/BaumannDignityRespect.pdf on May 10, 2025.

Bloom, P. (2016). *Against empathy: The case for rational compassion.* HarperCollins.

Bolman, L. G., & Deal, T. E. (2021). *Reframing organizations: Artistry, choice, and leadership* (7th ed.). Jossey-Bass.

Braaten, E. (2023). *Bright kids who couldn't care less: How to rekindle your child's motivation.* Guilford.

BrainyQuote. (n.d.). *John Maynard Keynes quotes.* Accessed at www.brainyquote.com/quotes/john_maynard_keynes_380219 on April 1, 2025.

Brantlinger, A. (2021). Entering, staying, shifting, leaving, and sometimes returning: A descriptive analysis of the career trajectories of two cohorts of alternatively certified mathematics teachers. *Teachers College Record, 123*(9), 28–56.

Canfield, J., & Hansen, M. V. (2001). *Chicken soup for the soul: 101 stories to open the heart and rekindle the spirit.* HCI Books.

Chapman, B., & Sisodia, R. (2015). *Everybody matters: The extraordinary power of caring for your people like family.* Portfolio.

Chenoweth, K. (2017). *Schools that succeed: How educators marshal the power of systems for improvement.* Harvard Education Press.

Conway, C. (2024). *Americans closely divided in terms of satisfaction with their local public schools, amid notable partisan gap, according to Marquette Law School pool survey*. Accessed at www.marquette.edu/news-center/2024/americans-closely-divided-in-terms-of-satisfaction-with-their-local-public-schools-amid-notable-partisan-gap.php on May 20, 2025.

Cooper, H. M., & Good, T. L. (1983). *Pygmalion grows up: Studies in the expectation communication process*. Longman.

Cottingham, B. W., Hough, H. J., & Myung, J. (2023). *What does it take to accelerate the learning of every child? Early insights from a CCEE school-improvement pilot*. Policy Analysis for California Education. Accessed at https://edpolicyinca.org/sites/default/files/2023-12/r_cottingham-dec2023.pdf on April 1, 2024.

Deal, T. E., & Kennedy, A. A. (1982). *Corporate cultures: The rites and rituals of corporate life*. Addison-Wesley.

De Cremer, D., & Mulder, L. (2007). *A passion for respect: On understanding the role of human needs and morality*. Accessed at www.researchgate.net/publication/227200909_A_passion_for_respect_On_understanding_the_role_of_human_needs_and_morality on May 10. 2025.

de Tocqueville, A. (2006). *Democracy in America* (J. P. Mayer, Ed.; G. Lawrence, Trans.). Harper Perennial Modern Classics. (Original work published 1835)

Drucker, P. (1992, September/October). The new society of organizations. *Harvard Business Review*, *70*(5), 95–104.

DuFour, R., DuFour, R., Eaker, R., & Many, T. (2006). *Learning by doing: A handbook for Professional Learning Communities at Work*. Solution Tree Press.

DuFour, R., DuFour, R., Eaker, R., Many, T. W., & Mattos, M. (2016). *Learning by doing: A handbook for Professional Learning Communities at Work* (3rd ed.). Solution Tree Press.

DuFour, R., DuFour, R., Eaker, R., Many, T. W., Mattos, M., & Muhammad, A. (2021). *Revisiting Professional Learning Communities at Work: Proven insights for sustained, substantive school improvement* (2nd ed.). Solution Tree Press.

DuFour, R., DuFour, R., Eaker, R., Many, T. W., Mattos, M., & Muhammad, A. (2024). *Learning by doing: A handbook for Professional Learning Communities at Work* (4th ed.). Solution Tree Press.

DuFour, R., & Eaker, R. (1998). *Professional Learning Communities at Work: Best practices for enhancing student achievement.* National Educational Service.

DuFour, R., & Fullan, M. (2013). *Cultures built to last: Systemic PLCs at Work.* Solution Tree Press.

DuFour, R., & Reeves, D. (2016). The futility of PLC lite. *Phi Delta Kappan, 97*(6), 69–71.

DuFour, R., Reeves, D., & DuFour, R. (2018). *Responding to the Every Student Succeeds Act with the PLC at Work process.* Solution Tree Press.

Eaker, R., & Keating, J. (2012). *Every school, every team, every classroom: District leadership for growing Professional Learning Communities at Work.* Solution Tree Press.

Eaker, R., & Keating, J. (2015). *Kid by kid, skill by skill: Teaching in a Professional Learning Community at Work.* Solution Tree Press.

Eaker, R., & Marzano, R. J. (Eds.). (2020). *Professional Learning Communities at Work and High Reliability Schools: Cultures of continuous learning.* Solution Tree Press.

Eastwood, K., & Seashore Louis, K. (1992, March). Restructuring that lasts: Managing the performance dip. *Journal of School Leadership, 2*(2), 212–224. https://doi.org/10.1177/105268469200200206

Edmondson, A. C. (2018). *The fearless organization: Creating psychological safety in the workplace for learning, innovation, and growth.* Wiley.

Edmondson, A. C. (2023). *The right kind of wrong: The science of failing well.* Atria Books.

EdTrust. (2021). *The importance of strong relationships between teachers and students.* Accessed at https://edtrust.org/rti/the-importance-of-strong-relationships on May 10, 2025.

Elevate Education. (2022). *How does the teacher shortage affect students?* Accessed at www.elevatek12.com/blog/elevate-in-action/how-does-the-teacher-shortage-affect-students on May 10, 2025.

Elmore, R. E. (2004). *School reform from the inside out: Policy, practice, and performance.* Harvard Education Press.

Empathy. (n.d.). In *Merriam-Webster's online dictionary.* Accessed at www.merriam-webster.com/dictionary/empathy on March 31, 2025.

Ericsson, K. A., & Pool, R. (2017). *Peak: How all of us can achieve extraordinary things.* Vintage.

Every Student Succeeds Act, 20 U.S.C. § 6301 (2015). Accessed at https://www.congress.gov/bill/114th-congress/senate-bill/1177 on February 21, 2025.

Fulton, K., & Britton, T. (2011, June). *STEM teachers in professional learning communities: From good teachers to great teaching.* National Commission on Teaching and America's Future. Accessed at https://files.eric.ed.gov/fulltext/ED521328.pdf on April 1, 2025.

Goleman, D., Boyatzis, R., & McKee, A. (2002). The emotional reality of teams. *Journal of Organizational Excellence, 21*(2), 55–65.

Good, T. L., & Brophy, J. E. (1980). *Educational psychology: A realistic approach* (2nd ed.). Holt, Rinehart & Winston.

Gould, S. J. (1996). *The mismeasure of man* (Revised and expanded ed.). Norton. (Original work published 1981)

Haasz, M., Boggs, J. M., Beidas, R. S., & Betz, M. E. (2022). *Firearms, physicians, families, and kids: Finding words that work*. Accessed at www.jpeds.com/article/S0022-3476(22)00478-4/fulltext on March 30, 2025.

Haidt, J. (2024). *The anxious generation: How the great rewiring of childhood is causing an epidemic of mental illness*. Penguin.

Hannah-Jones, N. (2021). *The 1619 project: A new origin story*. One World.

Hanson, H., Torres, K., Yoon, S. Y., Merrill, R., Fantz, T., & Velie, Z. (2021, August). *Growing together: Professional Learning Communities at Work generates achievement gains in Arkansas*. Education Northwest. Accessed at https://educationnorthwest.org/sites/default/files/plc-at-work-impact-evaluation.pdf on April 1, 2024.

Hattie, J. (2009). *Visible learning: A synthesis of over 800 meta-analyses relating to achievement*. Routledge.

Hattie, J. (2023). *Visible learning: The sequel—A synthesis of over 2,100 meta-analyses relating to achievement*. Routledge.

Hendry, J. (2013). *Management: A very short introduction*. Oxford University Press

Holt, J. (1964). *How children fail*. Pitman.

Ingersoll, R. M., Merrill, E., Stuckey, D., & Collins, G. (2018). *Seven trends: The transformation of the teaching force*. Accessed at https://files.eric.ed.gov/fulltext/ED593467.pdf on March 20, 2025.

Janks, M. (2024). *The five pillars of caring leadership*. Accessed at https://chapmancommunities.org/the-five-pillars-of-caring-leadership-building-a-foundation-for-thriving-teams/#:~:text=Caring%20leaders%20build%20trust%20through,concerns%20without%20fear%20of%20retribution on May 20, 2025.

Jimenez, K. (2023). *Most Americans are unhappy with the math taught in classrooms, new survey shows*. Accessed at www.usatoday.com/story/news/2023/04/17/families-unsatisfied-way-us-teaches-math/11666787002 on May 10, 2025.

Kenrick, D. T., Griskevicius, V., Neuberg, S. L., & Schaller, M. (2010). Renovating the pyramid of needs: Contemporary extensions built upon ancient foundations. *Perspectives on Psychological Science*, *5*(3), 292–314. https://doi: 10.1177/1745691610369469

King, M. L. Jr. (1958). *Stride toward freedom: The Montgomery story.* Harper & Row.

Korhonen, V. (2024, December 9). *Number of K–12 school shootings U.S. 1999–2024*. Statista. Accessed at https://www.statista.com/statistics/1463594/number-of-k-12-school-shootings-us/by on February 21, 2025.

Kouzes, J. M., & Posner, B. Z. (2011). *Credibility: How leaders gain and lose it, why people demand it* (Revised ed.). Jossey-Bass.

Kruger, J. S., Godley, S., & Heavy, S. C. (2021). Developing a culture of caring in classrooms: Best practices during a global pandemic and beyond. *Pedagogy in health promotion*, *8*(2), 99–103. https://doi:10.1177/23733799211051403

Lezotte, L. W. (1991). *Correlates of effective schools: The first and second generation*. Effective Schools Products.

Lezotte, L. W., & Snyder, K. M. (2011). *What effective schools do: Re-envisioning the correlates*. Solution Tree Press.

Lincoln, A. (1865). *Abraham Lincoln, second inaugural address*. Accessed at www.loc.gov/resource/mal.4361300/?st=text&r=0.019,-0.035,0.833,0.691,0 on February 23, 2025.

Lindblom, C. E. (1959, Spring). The science of "muddling through." *Public Administration Review*, *19*(2), 79–88.

Mankins, M., & Garton, E. (2017). *Time, talent, energy: Overcome organizational drag and unleash your team's productive power*. Harvard Business Review Press.

Many, T. W., Maffoni, M. J., Sparks, S. K., & Thomas, T. F. (2018). *Amplify your impact: Coaching collaborative teams in PLCs at Work*. Solution Tree Press.

Marshall, K. (2019, February 20). *Rethinking the way we coach, evaluate, and appreciate teachers*. Accessed at https://fordhaminstitute.org/national/commentary/rethinking-way-we-coach-evaluate-and-appreciate-teachers on October 2, 2024.

Marshall, K. (2024). *Teacher evaluation rubric*. Accessed at https://marshallmemo.com/marshall-publications.php#2 on May 21, 2025.

Marzano, R. J. (2001). *Classroom instruction that works: Research-based strategies for increasing student achievement*. ASCD.

Marzano, R. J. (2003). *What works in schools: Translating research into action*. ASCD.

Marzano, R. J. (2007). *The art and science of teaching*. ASCD.

Marzano, R. J., Pickering, D., & Pollock, J. E. (2001). *Classroom instruction that works: Research-based strategies for increasing student achievement*. ASCD.

Maslow, A. (1954). *Motivation and personality*. Harper.

Maslow, A. (1987). *Motivation and personality* (3rd ed.). Harper & Row.

McGonigal, K. (2015). *The upside of stress: Why stress is good for you, and how to get good at it*. Avery.

McGuffey, W. H. (1879). *McGuffey's third eclectic reader* (Revised ed.). Wiley & Sons. Accessed at www.gutenberg.org/files/14766/14766-pdf.pdf on April 1, 2025. (Original work published 1836)

Mercurio, Z. (2025). The power of mattering at work. *Harvard Business Review*, *103*(3), 100–109.

Mervosh, S., & Ngo, M. (2024, June 26). Why U.S. schools are facing their biggest budget crunch in years. *The New York Times*. Accessed at www.nytimes.com/2024/06/26/us/schools-budget-cuts-pandemic-aid.html on October 2, 2024.

Mineo, L. (2024). *Unfuzzy math: U.S. needs to do better*. Accessed at https://news.harvard.edu/gazette/story/2024/12/unfuzzy-math-u-s-needs-to-do-better on May 10, 2025.

mnmlscholar. (2023, May 12). *Of the easily communicated and challenging to use, a mnml digest*. Accessed at https://www.mnmlscholar.com/blog/5-2023-Of-the-easily-accumulated-and-challenging-to-use-a-mnml-digest on April 6, 2024.

National Academy of Education. (2024). *Evaluating and improving teacher preparation programs*. K. M. Zeichner, L. Darling-Hammond, A. I. Berman, D. Dong, & G. Sykes (Eds.). Accessed at https://naeducation.org/wp-content/uploads/2025/01/Evaluating_and_Improving_Teacher_Preparation_Programs.pdf on May 20, 2025.

No Child Left Behind Act of 2001, 20 U.S.C. § 6319 (2002).

Panchal, N. (2024, February 22). *The impact of gun violence on children and adolescents*. Kaiser Family Foundation. Accessed at www.kff.org/mental-health/issue-brief/the-impact-of-gun-violence-on-children-and-adolescents/#:~:text=Children%20living%20in%20areas%20with,disproportionately%20affects%20children%20of%20color. on March 30, 2025.

PDK International. (2024). *The 56th Annual PDK poll*. Accessed at https://pdkpoll.org on May 20, 2025.

Peetz, C. (2023, June 23). *Here's how educators feel about their safety at school*. Education Week. Accessed at www.edweek.org/leadership/heres-how-educators-feel-about-their-safety-at-school/2023/06 on March 25, 2025.

Peters, T. J., & Waterman. R. H. Jr. (2006). *In search of excellence: Lessons from America's best-run companies*. Harper.

Pfeffer, J., & Sutton, R. I. (2000). *The knowing-doing gap: How smart companies turn knowledge into action*. Harvard Business School Press.

Pondiscio, R. (2019). *How the other half learns: Equality, excellence, and the battle over school choice*. Avery.

Read on Arizona. (2024). *Case studies: Agua Caliente Elementary and Tanque Verde Elementary*. Accessed at https://readonarizona.org/case-studies/TVUSD on April 1, 2024.

Reeves, D. (2009). *Assessing educational leaders: Evaluating performance for improved individual and organizational results* (2nd ed.). Corwin.

Reeves, D. (2016). *From leading to succeeding: The seven elements of effective leadership in education*. Solution Tree Press.

Reeves, D. (2018). Seven keys to restoring the teacher pipeline. *Educational Leadership*, *75*(8). Accessed at www.ascd.org/el/articles/seven-keys-to-restoring-the-teacher-pipeline on April 1, 2025.

Reeves, D. (2020a). *The learning leader: How to focus school improvement for better results* (2nd ed.). ASCD.

Reeves, D. (2020b). Supercharged cabinet meetings: Establishing norms, recording commitments and requiring evidence for the body of senior leaders who advise the superintendent. *School Administrator*. Accessed at https://static1.squarespace.com/static/6043d8196805e2174276a15e/t/6043ea8d513b644d69a7a502/1615063693546/Supercharged+Cabinet+Meetings+April+2020.pdf on February 21, 2025.

Reeves, D. (2021a). *Deep change leadership: A model for renewing and strengthening schools and districts*. Solution Tree Press.

Reeves, D. (2021b). *Fearless schools: Building trust and resilience for learning, teaching, and leading*. Creative Leadership Press.

Reeves, D. (2023). *Fearless grading: How to improve achievement, discipline, and culture through accurate and fair grading*. Archway.

Reeves, D., & Eaker, R. (2019). *100-day leaders: Turning short-term wins into long-term success in schools*. Solution Tree Press.

Rimm-Kaufman, S., & Sandilos, L. (2025). *Improving students' relationships with teachers to provide essential supports for learning*. Accessed at www.apa.org/education-career/k12/relationships on May 10, 2025.

Rock, A. (2024, August 16). *Public school enrollment decline: Why students are leaving, where they're going, and why it matters.* Campus Safety. Accessed at www.campussafetymagazine.com/news/public-school-enrollment-decline-why-students-are-leaving/122644 on March 25, 2025.

Rogelberg, S. G. (2019). *The surprising science of meetings: How you can lead your team to peak performance*. Oxford University Press.

Rosenthal, R., & Jacobson, L. (1966). Teachers' expectancies: Determinants of pupils' IQ gains. *Psychological Reports, 19*, 115–118. Accessed at https://homepages.gac.edu/~jwotton2/PSY225/rosenthal.pdf on March 31, 2025.

Rubie-Davies, C. M. (2007). *Classroom interactions: Exploring the practices of high and low expectation teachers. British Journal of Educational Psychology, 77*, 289–306.

Rubie-Davies, C. M. (2008). Teacher beliefs and expectations: Relationships with student learning. In C. M. Rubie-Davies & C. Rawlinson (Eds.), *Challenging thinking about teaching and learning* (pp. 25–39). Nova.

Rubie-Davies, C. M., & Hattie, J. (2024). *The powerful impact of teacher expectations: A narrative review*. Accessed at www.tandfonline.com/doi/full/10.1080/03036758.2024.2393296#abstract on May 10, 2025.

Ryu, J., Walls, J., & Seashore Louis, K. (2020). Caring leadership: The role of principals in producing caring school cultures. *Leadership and Policy in Schools, 21*(3), 1–18. https://doi.org/10.1080/15700763.2020.1811877

Saphier, J., Haley-Speca, M. A., & Gower, R. (2008). *The skillful teacher: Building your teacher skills* (6th ed.). Research for Better Teaching.

Schmoker, M. (2004). Learning communities at the crossroads: Toward the best schools we've ever had. *Phi Delta Kappan, 86*(1), 84–88.

Senge, P. M., Ross, R. B., Smith, B. J., Roberts, C., & Kleiner, A. (1994). *The fifth discipline fieldbook: Strategies and tools for building a learning organization*. Doubleday.

Sheets, R. H., & Gay, G. (1996). Student perceptions of disciplinary conflict in ethnically diverse classrooms. *NASSP Bulletin, 80*(580), 84–94.

Sinek, S. (2009a, September). *How great leaders inspire action* [Video]. TED. Accessed at https://www.ted.com/talks/simon_sinek_how_great_leaders_inspire_action on February 21, 2025.

Sinek, S. (2009b). *Start with why: How great leaders inspire everyone to take action*. Portfolio.

Solution Tree. (2024a). *Evidence of excellence: Greater Hartford Academy of the Arts Middle School.* Accessed at www.solutiontree.com/plc-at-work/evidence-of-excellence/greater-hartford-academy on April 1, 2024.

Solution Tree. (2024b). *Evidence of excellence: Minnieville Elementary School.* Accessed at www.solutiontree.com/plc-at-work/evidence-of-excellence/minnieville on April 1, 2024.

Solution Tree. (2024c). *Evidence of excellence: Model PLC at Work and Blue Ribbon Schools.* Accessed at www.solutiontree.com/plc-at-work/evidence-of-excellence/model-plc-and-blue-ribbon-schools on April 1, 2024.

Solution Tree. (2024d). *Evidence of excellence: Pasadena Independent School District.* Accessed at www.solutiontree.com/plc-at-work/evidence-of-excellence/pasadena on April 1, 2024.

Solution Tree. (2024e). *Evidence of excellence: Tongue River Elementary School.* Accessed at www.solutiontree.com/plc-at-work/evidence-of-excellence/tongue-river-elementary on April 1, 2024.

Solution Tree. (2024f). *PLC at Work success story: Esther Starkman School (K–9).* Accessed at https://cloudfront-s3.solutiontree.com/pdf/EOE/SolutionTreeCAN_EstherStarkman.pdf?_ga=2.222595160.2104238624.1712243703-441923646.1689021104 on April 1, 2024.

Solution Tree. (2024g). *PLC at Work success story: Fern Creek High School.* Accessed at https://cloudfront-s3.solutiontree.com/pdf/EOE/SolutionTree_EOE_Fern_Creek.pdf?_ga=2.250626373.2104238624.1712243703-441923646.1689021104 on April 1, 2024.

Solution Tree. (2024h). *PLC at Work success story: Lake County Schools.* Accessed at www.solutiontree.com/plc-at-work/success-stories/lake-county on April 1, 2024.

Solution Tree. (2024i). *PLC at Work success story: Southeast Polk Community School District.* Accessed at www.solutiontree.com/plc-at-work/success-stories/southeast-polk on April 24, 2024.

Solution Tree. (2024j). *Solution Tree in Washington.* Accessed at www.solutiontree.com/st-states/washington on April 1, 2024.

Solution Tree. (2025). Maria Nielsen leans into the wind. *AllThingsPLC Magazine*, *9*(2), 17–22.

Stiggins, R. (2014). *Defensible teacher evaluation: Student growth through classroom assessment.* Corwin.

Stulberg, B. (2021). *The practice of groundedness: A transformative path to success that feeds—not crushes—your soul.* Penguin.

Suskind, D. (2015). *Thirty million words: Building a child's brain.* Dutton.

Suzuki, W. (2021). *Good anxiety: Harnessing the power of the most misunderstood emotion.* Atria Books.

Swift, J. (2017, September 6). *The curious history of slavery in Africa.* Accessed at https://research.cornell.edu/news-features/curious -history-slavery-west-africa on June 11, 2025.

Sympathy. (n.d.). In *Merriam-Webster's online dictionary.* Accessed at https://www.merriam-webster.com/dictionary/sympathy on March 31, 2025.

Taylor, F. W. (1911). *The principles of scientific management.* Harper.

Tierney, J., & Baumeister, R. F. (2019). *The power of bad: How the negativity effect rules us and how we can rule it*. Penguin.

Turkle, S. (2015). *Reclaiming conversation: The power of talk in a digital age*. Penguin.

U. S. Constitution. Amend. X, § 1.

Vogels, E. A. (2022, December 15). *Teens and cyberbullying 2022*. Pew Research Center. Accessed at https://www.pewresearch.org/internet/2022/12/15/teens-and-cyberbullying-2022/ on February 21, 2025.

Wiggins, A. (2018, February 28). *Lessons learned from shadowing students—Three years later*. Education Week. Accessed at www.edweek.org/education/opinion-lessons-learned-from-shadowing-students-three-years-later/2018/02 on October 2, 2024.

Will, M. (2023, December 21). *What will teacher shortages look like in 2024 and beyond? A researcher weighs in*. Education Week. Accessed at https://www.edweek.org/leadership/what-will-teacher-shortages-look-like-in-2024-and-beyond-a-researcher-weighs-in/2023/12 on February 21, 2025.

World Bank Group. (2021, December 6). *Learning losses from COVID-19 could cost this generation of students close to $17 trillion in lifetime earnings*. Accessed at www.worldbank.org/en/news/press-release/2021/12/06/learning-losses-from-covid-19-could-cost-this-generation-of-students-close-to-17-trillion-in-lifetime-earnings on October 2, 2024.

Yaeger, D. (2024). *10 to 25: The science of motivating young people: A groundbreaking approach to leading the next generation–And making your own life easier*. Avid Reader Press.

Yu, Y.-J. (2024). *US students' declining math scores are "sobering," expert says*. Accessed at https://abcnews.go.com/GMA/Living/us-students-declining-math-scores-sobering-expert/story?id=116481011 on May 10, 2025.

Zaki, J. (2019). *The war for kindness: Building empathy in a fractured world*. Crown.

Index

A

B

C

U

V

W

Y

Learning by Doing [Fourth Edition]

Richard DuFour, Rebecca DuFour, Robert Eaker, Thomas W. Many, Mike Mattos, and Anthony Muhammad

In this fourth edition of the bestseller *Learning by Doing*, the authors use updated research and time-tested knowledge to address current education challenges, from learning gaps exacerbated by the COVID-19 pandemic to the need to drive a highly effective multitiered system of supports.

BKG169

100-Day Leaders

Douglas Reeves and Robert Eaker

Within 100 days, schools can dramatically increase student achievement, transform faculty morale, reduce discipline issues, and much more. Using *100-Day Leaders* as a guide, you will learn how to achieve a series of short-term wins that combine to form long-term success.

BKF919

Leading PLCs at Work® Districtwide

Robert Eaker, Mike Hagadone, Janel Keating, and Meagan Rhoades

Ensure your district is doing the right work, the right way, for the right reasons. With this resource as your guide, you will learn how to align the work of every PLC team districtwide—from the boardroom to the classroom.

BKF942

JOY!

Timothy D. Kanold

Renowned educator Timothy D. Kanold takes readers through a mindful reflection of joy's significance in one's personal and professional life. Drawing on cultural concepts, insightful narratives, and brain research, he illustrates the discovery and conscious pursuit of joy to encourage reconnection with hope, purpose, engagement, and life balance.

BKG258